Praise for *Govern Agility*

"Organizational change is hard. Saying anything useful about how to go about it is hard. I don't know two people with more experience, integrity and honest reporting than Ponton and Gadzinski. They have tried all the easy ways and a variety of the hard ways, invented a number of creative ways, and can be trusted to tell you what works and what doesn't. Pay attention to their words, the words they avoid, the words that won't work, and the words they choose, those that have a chance. They have tried them all and have chosen their words carefully." *Dr Alistair Cockburn, Founding Co-Author of The Agile Manifesto*

"The authors provide a roadmap for reshaping governance practices in the digital age – the missing link in organizational transformations. *Govern Agility* merges agile principles into governance structures, offering practical insights and actionable strategies. With a focus on overcoming common challenges, it addresses the cultural shifts and mindset changes necessary for true organizational change. By dismantling traditional notions of corporate governance, it reveals a paradigm shift that is both refreshing and profoundly effective. The authors' ability to distil complex concepts into accessible and actionable insights is truly commendable. A compelling guide that is sure to leave a lasting impact on organizations worldwide."
Evan Leybourn, Co-Founder, Business Agility Institute

"I own a business rapidly growing towards medium. Editing *Govern Agility* exposed me to knowledge by Agile Governance thought-leaders. I was inspired. Thoughts percolated. I shared ideas and concepts with my team; sought their input. We now have solutions for one of the major problems of our size—I (the quality controller on which the business was built) had become a bottleneck. *Govern Agility* was a game-changer for us. Hawkeye has an increased sense of *us* and less *me.*" *Carolyn Martinez, Director, Hawkeye Publishing*

Praise for *Govern Agility*

"When that agile crowd got together in 2001 and crafted their manifesto, they had no idea the size of the bomb they were dropping on the IT industry. In the 20+ years since it was posted to the internet, the way we build and operate software projects and services has truly transformed. Technology departments are no longer money and time sinks that yield marginal value in the market. And agile is now more than a bundle of ideas for software teams. Its effectiveness can now be leveraged across the whole organization. Business agility is the new frontier; marketing, human resources, operations, and more. Wherever there are services and products, agile ideas can help make things better. But even as this agile goodness ripples out across the organization we're hearing voices of dissent, claims that agile is standing in the way of true progress… It's not agile that's the problem. It's the forest of old management systems and controls trying to hold onto outdated approaches. What do you want? Agility? Adaptability? Engaged, creative workforces? Or more of the same bureaucracy that drives 70% failure rates in projects by stifling innovation, generating extra work, and obfuscating clarity of purpose? Governance is a concept that is supposed to help teams and organizations stay on mission, get help when it's needed, and to change plans when necessary. Most governance groups are locked into "staying on mission". Some also monitor for risks, but rarely know what to do when they find them. Agile Governance ramps up clarity of mission, accountability, and adaptiveness… *Govern Agility* explores ideas and practices that can help transform not just our governance teams, but through their interactions and behaviors, will amplify the wins you get from your agile transformations by orders of magnitude."

Craig Brown, CEO, Everest Engineering

Govern Agility

Don't apply governance to your agile,
apply agility to your governance!

GADZINSKI & PONTON

HAWKEYE
PRESS

Published in Australia in 2024 by Hawkeye Press, an imprint of Hawkeye Publishing

Copyright © Phil Gadzinski & Tony Ponton 2024

Cover Design by Eli Southward

NATIONAL
LIBRARY
OF AUSTRALIA

A catalogue record of this book is available from the National Library of Australia.

ISBN 9781923105904

Proudly printed in Australia

www.governagility.com.au
www.hawkeyebooks.com.au

FOREWORD

Nobody sets out to create a bureaucracy, but without deliberate intervention our organizations always seem to inch towards it. The cost of removing controls, policies and procedures always seems higher than the cost of introducing them, and nobody ever got sacked for having too much governance.

The last decade has seen mainstream adoption of agile across many industries, but executives are asking why they aren't getting the promised results. The answer? You can spend millions of dollars training and coaching teams in agile approaches, but without changes to the boundary conditions in which they operate, you'll end up with largely the same outcomes.

Put simply, egalitarian work methods don't mix with authoritarian environments.

I've known and worked with Tony and Phil for nearly a decade. While many in the agile family were cutting their teeth in start-ups and scale-ups, Tony and Phil were working in large scale banks and telecommunications companies, and seeing first-hand the challenges of agility in highly regulated environments.

While others enjoyed working predominantly in the cloud on modern architectures, Tony and Phil were making continuous delivery work with green screens, mainframes and huge stored procedures that nobody understood. With funding processes that sucked the life out of ideas, and risk management processes that made accounting feel like some sort of extreme sport.

This book provides valuable guidance and real-world experience in how you can apply agile principles and values to the way that you govern your organization to make governance a value creator rather than simply a risk reducer.

Govern Agility is an important and valuable contribution to the business management landscape.

Andrew Blain, Founder Elabor8 (now a CPrime Company),
the Remote Agility Framework, and Flomatika

Table of Contents

PREFACE

When we wrote this book, we wanted to ensure that we portrayed the landscape of governance from what we have seen organizations experience and, more importantly, the foibles and frustrations of holding onto the methods of the past while attempting to move forward.

With that in mind, we have focussed the first few chapters on our observations of the world at large. We then provide insights into what we have learned, and techniques we have used, that help address this dynamic.

You will hear us refer to "we" a lot. Essentially, this is from either an experience we have had together, or one of us has had, and for ease we have made it a collective pronoun.

Thank you for choosing to read this book. It's our explicit hope that we provide you with the compass to guide you to a better way to enable your organization to deal with the new now and adapt to the next problems the future might throw at you.

Tony & Phil

1
What is Agile Governance?

In the early days of 2019, we were invited to work with a global organization that was struggling to meet their customers' needs. This was despite close to a century of history, culture, and deeply held traditions that drove their ways of working.

But maybe that was the problem. This organization maintained a classic, project-driven philosophy. They had long lead times and high levels of Work in Progress. The result was high overhead, high levels of waste, and little throughput—a typical 12-month funding cycle often took 18 months to bear fruit.

And as we dug deeper, more problems surfaced. Their teams were fragmented and siloed, working with disparate methodologies while poor communication and low transparency made it tough to get the data they needed to make decisions. Leadership was reminiscent of traditional approaches, focused on managing tasks rather than enabling teams. There were nods to more agile ways of working, but under the modern labels you found old-school administration. While there were pockets of strength and intent, the system was in conflict with itself.

Drawing threads between these symptoms pointed to one glaring problem: the lack of Agile Governance.

For those stepping into the world of agile for the first time, let's make sure we're all speaking the same language. We use the following definitions when discussing agile. Agile Governance is neither a framework nor a process. It is an intention, a series of questions to be asked, insights to be gained, and a frame of reference.

Agile (adjective): having the ability to move and change direction quickly, easily, and gracefully.

Dynamically Adaptive Organizations[1]: organizations that are dynamically evolving, changing, and adapting to meet the difficulties of the internal and external VUCA environments that enterprises must navigate every day in order to weather and thrive through the storms of disruption.

Governance[2]: the way that organizations or countries are managed at the highest level, and the systems for doing this: "Corporate Governance – we aim to promote and maintain the highest standards of directorship and corporate governance."

Agile Governance: applying the values and principles of agility to the way we govern an organization. In other words, ensuring the mechanisms, constraints, strategies, and delivery methods of the entire company are nimble and adaptive.

You're likely already familiar with the first term. Maybe even the second, if you've worked in the technology sector at any time over the past few decades. You may already know that agile originated in software development, and has subsequently evolved as a way of addressing the ever-changing demands of an increasingly volatile, uncertain, complex, and ambiguous (VUCA) world. You might even have encountered agile outside of software

[1] Ponton, T. (2023) https://www.remoteaf.co/insights
[2] Cambridge Dictionary sourced 6/11/2023
https://dictionary.cambridge.org/dictionary/english/governance

delivery. You don't have to be part of a technology development team to see the value in developing more flexible, responsive mindsets and methods.

Agile Governance, on the other hand, is still a relatively fresh concept even for agilists. It asks that we broaden our scope, widen our understanding beyond projects, teams, departments, or even release trains, and apply the fundamental concepts of agility to how we govern the system as a whole.

For many, it's a complicated mindset shift.

This book aims to make that shift a whole lot easier.

The big question is: why does Agile Governance matter? What does it provide that other methods of governance don't?

We just mentioned that the world is becoming increasingly VUCA – volatile, uncertain, complex, and ambiguous. We don't need to explain how economic, social, and political volatility have become the rule in the first half of the 21st century. As volatility increases, predictability drops, so it's no wonder that uncertainty is on the rise. Global interconnectivity is one of many factors increasing complexity, with more systems, more people and opinions, and more fingers tipping more scales. As for ambiguity, it seems that the more information we have at our fingertips, the harder it is to determine truth from fiction.

We'll dive further into VUCA later in this book. What matters for now is that Agile Governance enables integrity, transparency, and trust throughout your system of work which helps in addressing the challenges in navigating the modern VUCA world.

Agile Governance is achieved by moving the focus of working methods away from processes and tools, and towards individuals and interactions—this is, in fact, the first value of The Agile Manifesto[3]. Agile Governance accelerates information flow across

---

[3] The Manifesto for Agile Software Development. https://agilemanifesto.org/

the entire organization, rather than targeting specific teams or departments. This means that the time taken for an idea to become a decision, to become an action, and then to become an outcome, is minimized—crucial, when the world is changing faster than we can react to it. Or as an old colleague of ours used to say, "Problems change faster than we can develop and deploy the solutions to solve them".

Acceleration isn't a fresh concept to the seasoned agilist—agile ways of working have always had the capacity to build pace—yet not implementing modern governance along with modernizing your working systems eventually forces them to bow to traditional forms of governance, disempowering them and draining their autonomy. While acceleration and "moving at pace" are the current management buzzwords to drive things forward, in this case the old adage rings true: "The harder you push, the harder the system pushes back."[4]

In other words, if building agility within teams is like being handed the keys to a Ferrari, not using agile in your governance system is like driving without getting out of first gear.[5]

Agile Governance is far from the only form of governance that can enable your organization to function faster, more flexibly, and more transparently. For example, Lean Governance, which has its roots in the Lean Movement and TPS (Toyota Production System), has a strong genealogy, and is a governance method focused on streamlined structures and processes, which enables working together effectively to produce meaningful value for customers. It achieves this via oversight and decision-making regarding spending, auditing, and compliance measures, and by forecasting expenses and measurement. And all of these factors are important. However,

---

[4] Senge, P.M. (2006). The Fifth Discipline: the Art and Practice of the Learning Organization. New York: Doubleday/Currency
[5] Gadzinski and Ponton, Remote Governance, 2020

they aren't the totality of good Agile Governance. They seek to add governance to your agility. We want to add agility to your governance.

So how do we implement Agile Governance? That's a big question, and one we'll explore comprehensively throughout this book. In short, you can expect to need:

- Strong, enthusiastic leadership that communicates effectively;
- Commitment to distributed risk management;
- Buy-in across all levels of the organization;
- People across the organization who take responsibility for work and outcomes;
- Practice and implementation that keeps pace with intent.

Achieve this and you have the foundations of good Agile Governance. If not, you'll be struggling to benefit from the spontaneity and vision of humans, even from talented teams. It's often reflected that variability is what excites the intrapreneurs, giving you a competitive advantage. Without it, your people will find their dreams of empowerment, and the promise of human centricity that agile brings, slowly crumbling. Learned helplessness will prevail, and the organization will suffer. It will become reflective of the great five year planned economies of the soviet era, where the nation, and its subordinate (often invaded) satellite states, consisted of a rolling series of centralized economic plans, which were based on the Communist Party's theories of economic and social development.

We know where that leads!

If you're midway through this chapter and feeling as if Agile Governance is a radical departure from the governance frameworks you're used to, take comfort. Many organizations are already targeting Agile Governance, which often begins with agile-type transformations away from functional based silos and towards cross-functional teams. Call them tribes, domains, customer journeys, value streams, or release trains—they take many different forms. However, the fundamental purpose is the same: descaling and de-bureaucratizing the organization in pursuit of increasing speed of execution by removing barriers to change. This isn't the entirety of creating Agile Governance, but it is a great first step.

Is it possible to change structure in pursuit of agility and create more problems than you originally had? Of course. Is pursuing agility without properly re-thinking Agile Governance increasing risk to your transformation goals? Also, yes. Agile Governance looks complex. If it were simple, everyone would already be doing it. If you zoom out and look at the purpose and methodologies of Agile Governance from a distance, you'll see that it stands upon five simple stanchions (the definition of a **stanchion**[6] for this book is "a vertical pole used to support something"):

1. Conductive Leadership[7]—in essence, leaders conducting their teams like an orchestra, demonstrating clear intent, guiding their teams through decision-making, and standing ready to begin targeted interventions when problems arise. Creating harmony so their teams and their organization play in concert.

2. Sensible Transparency—to break down the walls of organizational silos, enabling transparency, open inquiry, greater alignment, and bi-directional information flow.

---

[6] (Stanchion Noun - Definition, Pictures, Pronunciation and Usage Notes | Oxford Advanced American Dictionary at OxfordLearnersDictionaries.com, n.d.)
[7] Leadership lessons from a symphony conductor: Itay Talgam at TEDxGateway 2013, https://www.youtube.com/watch?v=Mm8cASg_CQo

3. Patterns of Work—to redesign and codify ways of working across whole organizations in a way that enhances flow, distributes control, and ensures complete clarity of purpose and intent.

4. Data-Driven Reasoning—to collect, analyze and apply data using automated digital tools in a way that creates clarity, allows data to trump opinion, enables constant and continual improvement, and gets leaders out of their offices and down to the spaces where the work is being done.

5. Humanity—at the center of these four stanchions is a fifth stanchion that forms a cornerstone of Agile Governance: Humanity. Not cashflow, or productivity, or output. Humanity. To strip away artificial constraints and let people think and act independently, to communicate honestly, to fulfill the needs of their colleagues and customers, and to take pride in their accomplishments. To trust one another, to take responsibility, to align through democratic decision-making, to treat one another fairly, and to approach others with humility. We often see these statements as core values and principles plastered on the office wall, or the corporate intranet site, while the actual behaviors, controls, processes and actions inside organizations directly contradict them. Humanity as the cornerstone means living and embodying these values, not simply paying them lip service.

During the time we spent **crystallizing** ideas and writing this book, we had an ongoing and vigorous debate about the use of the term Stanchions: "a vertical pole used to support something". The metaphor relates to something being rigid and tending to have an enduring structure. Given we are talking about injecting agility into governance, and the core aspects of agility are movement and responsiveness, is it right to fix something? We think it is useful, as the Stanchions themselves are enduring containers where multiple practices and methods can reside and move, changing when the environment or the need changes. It's the anchor to change around. Maybe one day they will change as well.

Agile Governance is about changing the controls to reflect new ways of working and thinking. It places insights and opportunities into the hands of the entire organization, allowing for team, department, or whole-of-organization agility. It builds trust between leadership and teams, while using a data-driven feedback model to ensure that trust is well-placed. It lets people be people. And it paves the way to the promise of Enterprise agility.

There's nothing more important than that.

Let's return to our Global Organization from earlier in the chapter and imagine how an Agile Governance structure might have alleviated the challenges they were facing. Could smaller teams, arranged into tight and aligned teams of teams, have solved their siloing and collaboration issues? If management had been more versed in agile thinking, could they have put more effort into enabling their teams rather than micromanaging tasks? Would communication have become more transparent, helping them conquer their extended lead-times? Would greater visibility of work have improved trust between teams and leadership?

All of these concepts are interwoven. Building agility might begin with a single step, however you can't pluck at the thread of visibility to tighten up trust and call it a day. Creating visibility creates courage, but not all data points are equal or good. If you want to build true Agile Governance, you need to apply these new ways of thinking to the organization as a whole and allow all information to flow, good or bad.

That's crucial, because what some organizations mistakenly see as agile—changing team dynamics or implementing a new workplace tool—is a reductionist, simplistic approach to a complex adaptive system; a knee-jerk response to the new normal. They adapt piecemeal to the challenges of today without considering the potential of tomorrow. It's the window dressing of the problems you want, nay need, to solve.

New normal? It's an almost useless concept. Part of accepting the reality of a VUCA world is acknowledging that, by the time you've latched on to a new normal, it's already fading into irrelevance. What's more important is to build governance that's always ready for the *next normal.*

This requires considered and intentional organizational design, focused on creating or enhancing collaborative connective tissues. These tissues need to be able to respond to new strategies and opportunities quickly by pivoting structures and operating models in near-real time. This in turn enables communication, information flow, and maximizes the speed of directional decisions. Agile Governance, the governing of the system as a whole, is what enables this.

If you have watched the series, *The Witcher* [8](namely Season 3, Episode 3), you might remember this quote at the conclave from Geralt of Rivia when questioned on how he lives in a changing world and stays true: *"I shall continue on my path. I shall respond to events. I'll adapt with the world as it changes."*

We can't tell you what the next two, five, or ten years will bring. The future of global economics, politics, and business is as opaque to us as it is to you. We first learned how to make continuous delivery work with green screens, mainframes, and huge stored procedures when agile was still novel and being practiced by

---

[8] *The Witcher* (TV Series 2019–) | Action, Adventure, Drama. (2019, December 20). IMDb. https://www.imdb.com/title/tt5180504/

technologists only—anyone remember using AS400[9]? Look where we are now, how fast our sociotechnical world is changing. Agile is table stakes, and your mobile phone has more compute power than the first manned mission to space. In fact, the Apollo Missions' Guidance Computer's performance was comparable to the first generation of home computers from the late 1970s.

Moore's Law[10] seems to still have some relevance.

However, we can promise you that, by reading this book and applying the lessons within, you will be in a better position to adapt and thrive throughout the next normal (and the next, and the next).

Want to build true Agile Governance in your organization? We're ready to show you how.

---

[9] (IBM Archives: IBM AS/400, n.d.)

[10] Moore's law | Microprocessors, Transistors & Technology. (2023, November 10). Encyclopedia Britannica. https://www.britannica.com/technology/Moores-law

2

VUCA and the Modern World

Consider the world as it is today—economically, politically, technologically, and culturally. How much of a resemblance does it bear to the world of twenty years ago? How about ten years ago? Five? Two?

We used to be able to draw clear lines between decades marking major social shifts. Picture the eighties: a decade of excess, hard rock, huge hair, and the fall of the Berlin Wall. The 90s was a return to counterculture, the dotcom boom and bust, Tamagotchis and Y2K fears. But the 2000s? That's when it gets harder to pin down. As for the 2010s and '20s, it feels more and more like we're squeezing a decade's worth of innovation and industry upheaval into every eighteen months.

Demand for change is accelerating beyond our capacity to keep pace. Industry environments used to be stable for four to five years—enough time to read the market, set out a three-year plan, and execute it. Nowadays, you'd be lucky to get six months of stability regardless of your industry. This aligns with what we learned while working with the inestimable Rob Thomsett in the mid 2000s, not long after he wrote the book, *Radical Project Management*[11]. This book introduced the idea of eXtreme Project Management, and the concept of a shortening "window of

---

[11] https://www.amazon.com.au/Radical-Project-Management-Rob-Thomsett/dp/0130094862

15

stability", which describes the narrowing range of time you have before a previously defined problem changes into something new. It used to be that you had three to four years to understand, analyze, design, and build a market-ready solution to a problem. Now the problem changes before the original solution is even deployed.

This is why the market has often already moved on by the time a product is launched. The public have abandoned brand loyalty— they demand new and shiny innovations, improved services, and better prices, and they're nimble enough to shift providers on a whim. Brands still have power and presence, yet this can be undone in the blink of an eye with a data release that compromises customer privacy and security. For an example, see the class action lawsuit brought against Australian health insurance organization, Medibank Private, as a result of private customer information being leaked[12].

We once believed the earth was the center of the universe, until Copernican theory redefined how we saw ourselves in relation to the sun and stars. Likewise, the days of the customer coming begging to the organization are over. The world no longer revolves around the organization; the customer is the new center of the universe and the organization needs to come to them[13].

What happened to make the world this way? We could point our fingers at any number of culprits. Technological advances are the most obvious cause: global digitalization, the rise of artificial intelligence, and industrial robotization have accelerated every aspect of industry. As this evolved, customers have accelerated their expectations in turn, and in fact their expectations now transcend industries. On the other hand, we face a series of constant,

---

[12] Slater and Gordon. (n.d.). Medibank Data Breach Class Action. [online] Available at: https://www.slatergordon.com.au/class-actions/current-class-actions/medibank.
[13] Denning, S. (2018). The age of agile: how smart companies are transforming the way work gets done. New York: AMACOM.

overlapping and intersecting crises that make it harder and harder to meet these needs: climate change, financial crisis after financial crisis, the rise and fall of global superpowers…

Add all these factors together and you have a world that's increasingly VUCA: Volatile, Uncertain, Complex, and Ambiguous.

We can't go any further without laying the groundwork on VUCA: where the term comes from, what it means beyond the acronym, and how it affects the way we work and govern.

VUCA was first used in the mid-80s by economists and university professors, Warren Bennis and Burt Nanus, to describe the challenges and consequences of external factors upon corporate leadership[14]. If only they'd known how much more VUCA things would become over the following decades!

VUCA then became used by the US Army War College to describe the political, social, and military environment after the collapse of the Soviet Union. The old-world order of predictable cause and effect behaviors was gone. Prisoner swaps on Berlin's Glienicke Bridge were swept away in an overwhelming wave of Perestroika and Glasnost.

In the early 2000s, VUCA once again found a foothold outside the military. With the fears and doubts of Y2K in the rear-view mirror, tech development and big data accelerated. With that acceleration came fresh challenges in an exponentially complex and interdependent world.

The foot never lifted from the pedal. VUCA is everywhere. Go to any agile or ways-of-working conference and every speaker will kick off their presentation with a spiel about the world being a VUCA environment (in fact, we do it all the time). When consultants roll into your organization to tell you why you need

---

[14] Bennis, W.G. and Nanus, B. (2012). Leaders: the Strategies for Taking Charge. New York: Harperbusiness.

another agile transformation, what they will likely follow with is, "You need to be able to thrive in a VUCA world."

Let's break VUCA down into its component parts:

V = Volatility: the nature and dynamics of change, and the nature and speed of change forces and change catalysts.

U = Uncertainty: the lack of predictability, the prospects for surprise, and the sense of awareness and understanding of issues and events.

C = Complexity: the multiplex of forces, the confounding of issues, no cause-and-effect chain and confusion that surrounds organization.

A = Ambiguity: the haziness of reality, the potential for misreads, and the mixed meanings of conditions; cause-and-effect confusion.

In a VUCA environment, each of these four elements can present in different ways and intensities. They can intersect, interact, and amplify one another. They can manifest slowly over time or disrupt an entire industry with the subtlety of a brick through a window. VUCA can be intrinsic, inside your organization, as well as extrinsic, outside of it. Just as a global market can be volatile, uncertain, complex, or ambiguous, so can your own internal processes, relationships, departments, funding, confidence levels, and so on.

A simple way to visualize VUCA is by considering taking a group of friends out for lunch. If we need to drive, that could mean a lot of traffic, increasing complexity. The weather is growing increasingly foggy, making the driver uncertain. The passengers want to know when they'll get there… but where is there? Nobody knows where they want to eat, or even what's available. Ambiguity is high. Since everyone wants to get there immediately, the car is always accelerating. Any little twitch of the wheel could result in a loss of control. This volatile situation will require steady hands, the ability to read the ebb and flow of traffic, a deep understanding of how the car functions (and how far it can be pushed before it loses traction or explodes), and a readiness to adapt to the changing needs of the passenger. An experienced driver, practiced and disciplined in their approach, is able to better adapt to the changing conditions. A newly licensed driver, or one with a fixed approach to operating a vehicle, may not be able to make the changes necessary to meet those conditions.

Just like our hypothetical driver, organizations must prepare to make fast decisions and respond to the events and boundaries that arise from VUCA environments. This is especially important when thinking about governance. Traditional and fixed governance are typically designed to be efficient and effective in stable, predictable environments. In a VUCA world, traditional governance freezes like a kangaroo in the headlights.

However, the same factors causing some governance models to panic and seize up will allow other models to succeed. Take information flow, for example. This acceleration in change has caused an explosion in available data and information. Ironically, traditional governance models are drowning in data yet don't have the technology, time, or skill sets to generate useful insights from it. That's doubly frustrating for those who crave certainty and detail before moving forward. However, for those who can make sense of that data, who can pick those insights out of the information soup, who can take small steps forward while waiting for the fog to clear—they have the capacity to not just survive, but to thrive.

When it comes to making sense of this VUCA environment, we often begin with the Cynefin Framework. We'll dive into this framework in greater detail later in the book, but for now all you need to know is that the Cynefin Framework[15] acts as a guide to support leaders, and sense the environmental context they are in. This helps them make better decisions using models that fit the problem they are trying to solve. There are five specific contexts in which leaders need to learn how to act appropriately[16]:

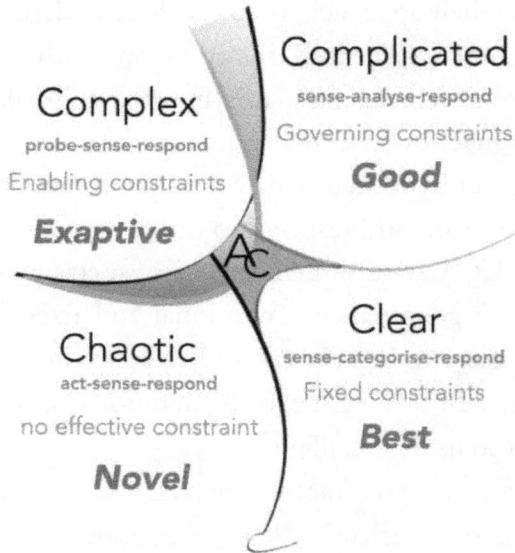

[15] Snowden, D. and Boone, M. (2007). A Leader's Framework for Decision Making. [online] Harvard Business Review. Available at: https://hbr.org/2007/11/a-leaders-framework-for-decision-making.
[16] The domains we operate in: About - Cynefin Framework - The Cynefin Co
[17] (2023) The Cynefin Framework. Available at: https://thecynefin.co/about-us/about-cynefin-framework/

- Chaotic: where everything is upside-down. Complete disorder and unpredictability reigns, and the priority is to stabilize the situation, establish constraints, and then transition the problem to one of the other, less chaotic domains.

- Complex: where problems are dynamic and unpredictable, and the cause-and-effect relationship behind those problems is not immediately apparent. In this context, the focus shifts from analysis to experimentation and adaptation, where we probe, sense, and respond to emergent patterns.

- Complicated: where problems are more intricate and require expertise to analyze and solve. This domain calls for the input and support of experts, and solutions may involve multiple perspectives, research, and analysis.

- Clear: also known as the Simple domain, problems here are well-defined and have clear cause-and-effect relationships. The best approach is to apply known best practices and standardized processes to achieve predictable outcomes.

- Confused: also known as Disordered. Confused is a state that can exist in any of the other domains. It implies we don't actually know which domain we are in or how to approach a problem. It is crucial to recognize when you are in a state of Confusion and to take the necessary steps to shift to a more appropriate domain.

Using a framework like Cynefin helps us navigate a VUCA world. It becomes possible to better understand the nature of problems and distinguish between those which may already have tried and tested solutions and problems for which there may be no existing solutions. In these cases, it's often more effective to probe, sense, and then respond to the problem; to learn by doing. We know that in the digital age, it's the organizations that learn the fastest that will succeed. Cynefin provides us with a path from the unknown to the known, and gives leaders the tools to move problems between domains until they can efficiently solve them repeatedly.

Frameworks also help us place ourselves within these environments, providing a better understanding of which forces we can influence, which we can't, which methods we can retain, which need to change, and so on.

Just as the car traveling at breakneck speed down a foggy highway can solve its problems incrementally (slow down a little! turn on the high beams! explore the passengers' needs to better orient yourself toward a destination!), organizations can do the same. However, we can't just adjust our traditional governance models to make them VUCA-ready. There's no amount of tweaking that will make these models future-fit.

Traditional governance models are designed for a clear world where best practices and constraints are used as effective solutions to known problems. How can you apply best practices before you have a solution or, in some cases, before you've even defined the problem? These complex, chaotic worlds demand a more nimble (or, could we say, agile?) approach.

This is where the distinction between investing time and effort into agile ways of working and **Agile Governance** becomes more pronounced. Many organizations, when embracing a move to agile ways of working, dive in without considering the broader picture. They break people out of their boundaries into new constraints like tribes, squads, etc. and hand down new ways of working to their employees without giving them the time to get to know their new teams or decide how they want to work. They copy agile models from other organizations without understanding the context that made those models successful. Most critically, they fail to address the tension between these new ways of doing the work and existing ways of governing the work. They forget that the models they are seeking to emulate have evolved from years, if not decades, of learning and adaptation. However, it's hard to sell decades of learning and adaptation as the solution, so…

The result: agile(ish) teams trapped in an old governance system that limits transparency and devalues trust. Teams ready and willing to adapt to changing markets being forced to work according to monthly status reports. Innovators constrained by top-down decision-making having to write investment cases to free funds for solutions to problems they have barely defined. In these situations, leadership will see control of the environment slipping through their fingers (as agility by its very nature is designed to disseminate control) and often respond by amplifying the worst of those old methods in order to claw back their authority. The harder you push, the harder the system pushes back[18]. This is only amplified in VUCA environments, where the natural response to uncertainty is to tighten the reins by upping governance.

Why are leaders so keen to respond to VUCA situations by increasing controls instead of investigating the root causes, and using agility to solve their foundational problems? One theory is that much of our management attended the same schools and universities, emerged with the same training, and created a systemic tendency towards certain patterns of thinking. Today's leaders largely learn the same principles that emerged from Taylorism, the

---

[18] Senge, P.M. (2006). *The Fifth Discipline: The Art and Practice of the Learning Organization.* London: Random House Business

principles or practice of scientific management and work efficiency as practiced in a system known as the Taylor System. This system remains a staple of MBA courses. Taylorism has now rebranded itself as Six Sigma, Business Process Engineering, and so on, however, the underlying principles are the same: a focus on precise mechanical control of human endeavor to optimize for physical labor.

Another perspective is that we get so myopic in large organizations—we navel gaze, tending to see a different ecosystem and performance than external viewers—that we lose sight of what good looks like. We become unable to interpret the weak signals that are all around us as information for decision-making, or we don't even have access to this information. In fact, there is so much information and so little time that we don't know which signals to respond to and how, so we put more controls in place. We do this so frequently and build so many layers of controls that nobody even understands why they are used other than simply because that is how they have always been used. We follow processes and tools over individuals and interactions; the agile order is flipped.

Career transformation coaches hit identical failure points across multiple organizations and industries, wherein asking the leadership group to change is a steeper challenge than changing the organization as a whole. There is also a (valid) school of thought that many people crave certainty. Uncertainty is uncomfortable, and many struggle to hold themselves in that state, even if in the pursuit of something important to them. We have seen this emerge even in the most confident and experienced leaders, where being trapped in uncertainty quickly becomes unbearable.

We often blame the system for rejecting change, but the system is just a collection of humans working towards a common goal, and all those humans want to survive.[19] Leaders are faced with an unenviable choice: alter their behavior to match the emerging needs of their increasingly autonomous teams or meet the rigid demands of legacy governance frameworks.

Adapting yourself to the system is sometimes a pathway to organizational survival. Added to this are the overall demands and burdens on leaders, which have grown exponentially over the last few decades. The often-conflicting priorities and directions, regulations and customer expectations, never-ending threats and opportunities, as well as the explosion in cyber challenges, artificial intelligence, and technology revolutions, make it impossible to keep pace with a working understanding of all these concepts at once. Yet, our systems demand that our leaders do so, and we wonder why burnout and mental health issues are on the rise.

These leaders are working within a rigid system that refuses to see itself as the problem. As per Maslow's Law of the Instrument: "I suppose it is tempting, if the only tool you have is a hammer, to treat everything as if it were a nail."[20] Traditional governance is the hammer, and when things go wrong, the typical response is to first blame the nail (or screw, or drill-bit) and then fetch more hammers.

This brings us back to the need for new governance models. Agile ways of working are insufficient in a VUCA world unless framed by a more holistic, systemic governance approach designed for an organization's specific context, where leaders are willing to step away from tradition and embrace novelty. We need

---

[19] Kahneman, D. (2011). Thinking, Fast and Slow. New York: Farrar, Straus and Giroux.

[20] Ellis, S. (2023, March 2). *"If the only tool you have is a hammer, you tend to see every problem as a nail." — The Fitzrovia Psychology Clinic.* The Fitzrovia Psychology Clinic. https://thefitzroviaclinic.com/if-the-only-tool-you-have-is-a-hammer-you-tend-to-see-every-problem-as-a-nail/

lightweight, dynamic, and adaptive systems that provide faster feedback in risk and compliance; flexible models that are willing to start small and welcome change.

Let's put the hammer down. Better yet, let's buy a whole new toolbox.

Let's talk about Agile Governance.

3

What is Governance?

Before we can dive into *how* to inject agile into governance, we need to take the time to describe, at a much deeper level, what we believe governance is. For our purposes, we are more focused on corporate governance, the way that organizations need to be governed, rather than broader theories of governance itself. There is no single conclusive definition of corporate governance, but if you take a global view, there are common overarching themes that we will focus on for discussing Agile Governance.

In the United States[21] for example: *The corporate governance system is best understood as the set of fiduciary and managerial responsibilities that binds a company's management, shareholders, and the board within a larger, societal context defined by legal, regulatory, competitive, economic, democratic, ethical, and other societal forces.*

The Organization for Economic Co-operation and Development (OECD)[22] defines governance in these terms: *Corporate governance involves a set of relationships between a company's management, its board, its shareholders, and other stakeholders. Corporate*

---

[21]Oregon State University; The US Corporate Governance System; sourced 06/01/2023;
https://open.oregonstate.education/strategicmanagement/chapter/2-the-u-s-corporate-governance-system/
[22] OECD Principles of Corporate Governance; Sourced 06/11/2023;
https://www.oecd.org/corporate/principles-corporate-governance/

governance also provides the structure through which the objectives of the company are set, and the means of attaining those objectives and monitoring performance are determined.

The Governance Institute of Australia[23], for example, defines it in these terms: *Governance encompasses the system by which an organization is controlled, and operates and the mechanisms by which it and its people are held to account. Ethics, risk management, compliance, and administration are all elements of governance.*

The ASX Corporate Governance Council goes a little further: *The phrase "corporate governance" describes "the framework of rules, relationships, systems and processes within and by which authority is exercised and controlled within corporations. It encompasses the mechanisms by which companies, and those in control, are held to account."[24] (In fact, this definition was drawn from Justice Owen in the HIH Royal Commission, **The Failure of HIH Insurance** Volume 1: A Corporate Collapse and Its Lessons, Commonwealth of Australia, April 2003, at page xxxiv.) Good corporate governance promotes investor confidence, which is crucial to the ability of entities listed on the ASX to compete for capital.*

Okay, but What Does That Mean?

Let's boil this down to the essentials by thinking about governance and how it applies to the ways in which we work. Governance is, at its root, about how we intend to govern our systems, what we use to control those systems, and how we can provide assurances those controls are actually working as many large-scale organizations are not run by the people that own them, creating a need for broader

---

[23] Governance Institute of Australia; sourced 06/11/2023; https://www.governanceinstitute.com.au/resources/what-is-governance/;
[24] ASX; Corporate Governance Principles and Recommendations; ASX Corporate Governance Council Third Edition; March 2014

controls. As for systems, we are largely referring to the social and organizational systems that people create when they come together around things, as opposed to the more common usage of systems regarding technological systems. Within this context, Governance also includes monitoring and controlling the execution of strategy with the whole system of work in mind. Strategy left ungoverned becomes words on a page, and the work executed becomes unaligned to the strategy. Then we see drift and waste emerge across the organization—we do work that's not valued and not effective and doesn't get us to our goal.

You are likely already familiar with traditional governance, which relies on extensive planning and heavyweight control mechanisms in order to keep systems running as intended. Agile Governance has the same root definition and all the same foundations as traditional governance: to consider how processes, interactions, and controls enable outcomes, but seeks to do this in a more flexible, adaptable, and agile manner. It's not just about project management offices and processes; it's about reimagining how you govern your entire system of work at all levels to enable your organization's success.

Like traditional governance, Agile Governance values planning yet is flexible and adaptive, enabling the ability to change the plan to suit the situation as more information emerges. As such, it is better suited to support responding to change when prior plans lose relevance in the face of VUCA. We see that the fundamental difference between traditional and Agile Governance is that traditional governance models assume that the future can be predictably determined and that we need to govern the execution of plans to take us towards that future, whereas Agile Governance assumes that the future is uncertain and that we need to govern the decisions, actions, behaviors, etc. that will allow us to find the best path forward.

29

You may have already heard of Agile Governance, which is described as oversight and decision-making of spending, audit, and compliance, or perhaps forecasting expenses and measurement. There are also a number of models touted by consultancies and scaling frameworks as plug-and-play panaceas to solve your governance woes. These models can be useful, but they generally err towards processes, tools, and documentation rather than exploring the whole of the model and how we control the situation. In the words of George Box, "Essentially, all models are wrong, but some are useful." While this quote was related to statistical models, the analogy still applies. Regardless, we would struggle to label those sorts of models as governing with agility.

To better understand what we think of as Agile Governance, let's revisit those original definitions. We see that governance is a stated outcome of the process of interactions through laws, norms, power, and language. Meanwhile, one of the key values of the Agile Manifesto is: "Individuals and interactions over processes and tools." So, governance and agility aren't in opposition. By definition, they support one another, so long as we ensure that interactions are taking precedence over processes. As shown in each of the four values of the Agile Manifesto, we do mean "over" and not "in place of".

The idea of a larger societal context could refer to a community, a family, an organization, or anything in between. However, the word organized, in particular, implies a structure, a system of control. Some agilists might recoil at the mention of controls—they shouldn't! Control isn't a dirty word. However, we all probably have some experience with bad controls (like weekly audits and reports) put in place by leadership as a reflexive reaction to their distance from the work being done. We could argue that these leaders don't actually want to control their direct reports. What they want is an assurance that everything is functioning as intended, and the customer is being served.

This may be, in part, due to an element of trust or, more accurately, distrust. Many people struggle to trust what they've been told, thanks to bad experiences. Other times, distrust forms the basis of their overarching mental model and bias. Many companies exhibit low-trust cultures, and you will often find higher degrees of process and centralized control in these archetypes. The answer is not to trash the concept of control, but to reconsider what controls need to be put in place for what problem, what context, audience, and so on.

Let's also examine who is doing this governance: the government of a state, a market, or a network. One of the values of the Agile Manifesto is "customer collaboration over contract negotiation". When we collaborate with customers, we create mutually supportive networks. Therefore, it is fundamentally agile to build a system of governance driven by our relationships with our customers.

Some may take exception to us reinterpreting the Agile Manifesto in this way in order to serve our concept of Agile Governance. We would argue that the Manifesto is twenty years old, as of our writing, and must be subject to interpretation and adaptation. Otherwise, how can it be agile? In fact, Dr. Alistair Cockburn, a prime initiator of the agile movement, considers the Manifesto an artifact of that period in time, which must be added to in order to remain relevant for changing contexts. It was relevant for the domain at the time and the problems the cosigners were facing, but now?

This mirrors the events of the First Council of Nicaea in AD 325. Emperor Constantine herded 300 arguing bishops into a single location to resolve their differences and align on a single, unified

Christian doctrine[25]. That same doctrine still forms the foundation of the Orthodox and Catholic churches, yet many denominations build upon this doctrine in a way that suits their community and needs. So, too, must we add what we need to the Manifesto in order to keep pace with the world of today. If you need evidence that the founding signatories of the Agile Manifesto believe this too, then check their actual page with the values and principles. https://agilemanifesto.org/. It has remained unchanged since Ward Cunningham posted it on the web in 2001! Except for adding language translations and signatories, the latter also stopped because the number of signatories became too hard to track. We do note that we got in early and were listed in time. Many, however, have not only built doctrines on top of it; they have created industries around it.

The final part of the intent—the simplification of governance to political processes within and between institutions—is a little trickier. It's an accurate definition, yet one that we wish wasn't necessarily true. Governance creates, amplifies, and thrives upon politics within and around organizations. Politics creates power and authority, and in many organizations, we mistakenly invest power into governance, thus taking it away from the teams doing the actual work. How often do we treat processes driven by governance and controls as dogma?

Many years ago, while attending an agile training course with Dr. Alistair Cockburn, we ran an exercise around developing a walking skeleton backlog. We broke into small groups to tackle a problem with a very ambiguous direction. Within the space of a minute, there were already arguments arising about sticking to specific processes, even when a process hadn't been defined! We

---

[25] For more information, see (2019). First Council of Nicaea | Description, History, Significance, & Facts. In: Encyclopædia Britannica. [online] Available at: https://www.britannica.com/event/First-Council-of-Nicaea-325.

went from idea to solution to process to dogma in the blink of an eye. Humans seem to be hardwired to look for a pathway to follow and ease the burden of thinking. Dr. Cockburn himself summed it up for us that day: "Process is just someone else's good trick."

Human nature tends to try to conserve energy by simplifying pathways. Where change is hard and can often be painful, we see that scenario emerge time and again where process becomes the arbiter of progress. Given governance traditionally tends to encourage fixed process, policy, and constraints, it clearly speaks to some innermost needs and perhaps even the essence of humanity to make life easier the next time around.

The relationship between politics and governance is a function of how humans rely upon norms, structures, and behaviors to create a sense of control and stability (both within organizations and otherwise). However, the pursuit of control and stability can go too far. How many of us have seen an organization that defines itself so concretely that they can't imagine stepping outside the walls of their domain? Or in which they've lost the sense of connection between their services/product functions and the solutions their customers are asking for? Mission statements like, "*We do X or We are Y*" can help an organization ground itself. But when those statements become enforced through rigid governance, things can get hairy.

We see this problem manifesting in how many large organizations now embark on customer revolutions, customer centricity transformation, or anything to do with remembering or reconnecting to its reason for existence, i.e. the customer. Governance is often a symbol or a symptom of this. When we see this, we often revisit Peter Drucker's thoughts on organizations: "The purpose of a business is to create and keep a customer." Ironically, it's not the front-line staff forgetting this. Employees in brick and mortar or service industries stay close to the customer and know how to serve them. It's the people in the back offices, or organizations with digital-only functions, who often don't know who their customers are or what they need.

Let's jump back to that definition one final time. Governance is a construct of the decision-making and decision-making delegation among the actors involved in a collective problem. In other words, governance should be formed by the people actively solving problems and getting involved in decision-making. So why do we so often see governance dictated by people outside or above those circles? What could we achieve if we put governance back in the hands of the people getting the work done? We would argue that successful governance should be distributed and take authority to the work without sacrificing control levers. Good governance, agile or otherwise, demands a sense of responsibility and ownership from everyone, which allows for greater levels of trust and, in turn, higher performing teams. What we tend to see though, is the continued manifestation of Taylorist thinking transferring the manufacturing context to knowledge work: separation of workers from management. With this mindset, it makes sense to keep governance as a separate activity. However, much of the knowledge workplace is not a factory anymore.

Who Does Governance Serve?

That's a tricky question. It's better to break it down into two parts: who does governance serve *now*, and who *should* governance serve if done correctly?

In the context of this book, governance serves several stakeholders. In traditional settings, that makes the primary beneficiaries of governance and the people demanding it the shareholders of the company and the broader community, which expects the upholding of cultural standards. We often include employees in this, given the impact on people of organizational decisions. That's why we have HR policies. The formal leadership group of the organization responds to this expectation by setting strategy, determining direction, bearing responsibility for problems, and reaping the rewards of success. They're the people who, in the case of publicly listed organizations, have to report to shareholders on matters of investment, capital, trends, margins, returns on investment, and so on. They're also the ones who have to comply with government and industry regulations.

A large part of creating successful Agile Governance requires us to rethink the role leadership plays in governing the work, and the system. Traditional hierarchical management theory X-style leadership[26] doesn't like to distribute authority out of fear of eroding their power base. In other words, we can't create Agile Governance or serve those closest to the work using classical methods. Yet the move to Holacracy[27] and totally distributed governance with no traditional hierarchy doesn't seem to succeed either.

If we want to create modern governance, we must begin with modern leadership principles.

Why Do We Need and Ask for Governance?

In traditional organizations, governance may, to those who suffer the worst of its excesses, be the boogeyman. A system of constraints and audit processes that restrict creativity, autonomy, and service of the customer.

It's critical that you don't get that impression from what we've

---

[26] theory X and theory Y. (n.d.). Oxford
Reference. https://doi.org/10.1093/oi/authority.20110803103840351
[27] Holacracy - The Management Framework for a Complex World. (n.d.).
Holacracy Foundation. https://www.holacracy.org/

explored so far in this chapter. We need governance. We beg for governance. However, we want *good* governance. We want governance that enables autonomy with directional alignment; that empowers interconnected networks of people and teams who all have the ability to respond to emerging changes and needs. We want governance that empowers and uplifts. We want governance that creates opportunity.

The problem is that governance is often structured around a few critical concerns: ensuring that the organization is meeting its obligations (to shareholders, partners, governments, etc.) and can continue to trade. This results in a lot of governance being directed by external third parties, who mandate regular audits to ensure that the organization is actually doing what it says it's doing. This type of governance focuses on ensuring accurate information can flow to other stakeholders, and that this information can be relied upon when making decisions. This large-scale, outside-in governance is then distributed and filters down through the organization in the form of cultures, behaviors, and processes.

Again, we reiterate that external governance is good. A world without regulatory standards is a terrifying prospect. The free market doesn't always get it right, and society imposes constraints on organizations to protect the consequences of unfettered ambition. We regularly see examples where, even with tight controls, there is exploitation of the "gray"—that area not quite fully covered by regulation—or where an industry or product has moved faster than the regulator can keep up with, to detrimental, damaging, and sometimes life-threatening effects from the use or the creation of a product or service. There are always examples of unbudgeted externalities. Externalities can be considered unpriced goods involved in either consumer or producer market transactions: the external cost (or benefit) to others. Air pollution from motor vehicles is one example. The cost of air pollution to society is not paid by either the producers or users of motorized transport but by all of society.

The issue arises when we begin to believe (and we'd argue that we've become culturally predisposed to this view) that this sort of governance must be applied heavily and broadly, from the top down.

The result of this culture is the creation of an entire industry dedicated to governance, auditing, and controls. The vast amounts of money being spent on ensuring governance demands (by, for example, regulators, markets, shareholders, etc.) have resulted in enormous amounts of power being concentrated in the hands of auditing services. We see, given this static aspect, a static governance approach—does anyone remember during the heights of Covid being demanded, by regulatory bodies, to still physically sign, and have someone physically witness, a deed?

So, what choice do organizations have if they want to keep serving their customers? No wonder the largest consultancy firms around the world have their roots in audit and compliance work.

In other words, our relationship with governance is not always healthy. It's becoming increasingly necessary to reexamine what we actually want from our governance and how we can make it work for us.

Let's ask a simple question then: why do we want systems that ensure the work is getting done properly?

The answer: to reduce risk.

Kent Beck, Agile Manifesto co-signer and creator of Extreme Programming[28], described it well: "Silence is the sound of risk piling up." When we don't know where work is happening, what work is happening, or why it's happening, we invite risk.

---

[28] Beck, K. (2004). *Extreme programming explained: embrace change*. Boston, Mass.: Addison-Wesley.

In fact, what is often misunderstood about agile methods and thinking is that, if applied with discipline, it results in early risk reduction of human endeavor. Adopting agile is about more effectively managing the risk of change. This often confounds many new to agile folk—the dichotomy of discipline with degrees of freedom. If you can see it early, you can manage it: the iterative nature of agility enables it to serve as an early warning system. We have never spoken to any leader who didn't want to see and understand risk early. In short, it's the attitude you bring to the problem domain. As Dr. Alistair Cockburn will often say, "agile is your attitude."

What can compound that risk? Delays in elevating information, or wrong decisions that cause or increase misalignment. There's a theory that we use often, that we each make hundreds of decisions or more per day, and that number has been increasing exponentially over the last decade.[29] However, for the sake of argument, let's say that individuals in teams make ten decisions every day that impact the team's direction. Five days in a week, forty-six working weeks in a year... that's 2,300 potentially wrong decisions per person, per year. Each bad decision compounds upon the last. Add to that a truncated or delayed information flow, and the impact of those mistakes becomes exponential. Worse still, the solution is often to turn to the highest-paid person in the room for an answer to this rapidly accelerating problem... and their solution is often based on gut feel when they are likely the furthest removed from the problem itself. Then, just to rub salt in the wound, they'll propose additional controls in order to avoid repeating the same mistakes, not realizing that the controls were often the root cause!

Why does this continue to happen even in purportedly agile

---

[29] D. K Analytics; sourced 06/11/2023; 14,250 people surveyed in January 2023; https://www.prnewswire.com/news-releases/global-study-70-of-business-leaders-would-prefer-a-robot-to-make-their-decisions-301799591.html

organizations? One argument is that many organizations undergoing agile transformations are not actually transforming, only becoming transitional. Their "transformations" are generally concentrated upon changing patterns of work, with the majority of resources going into the team level. There's a little left over for the funding and governing level, and nothing left at all for transforming systems, strategy, and leadership. Worse still, we often find that the transformations on the team level versus funding and governing are working in opposition to one another. The result is a three-tier transformation that results in further misalignment. Often these transformations are about the people doing the work only—an unfortunate return to Taylorist thinking—because they *must* be the problem! If only people could be more productive, all our issues would be solved... or so some people would like to believe.

This is the nature of traditional governance when applied to "hidden" work like technology and software development. It employs Taylorist, production-line thinking to what are fundamentally creative endeavors. It assumes that creating a product is a checklist of processes that can be controlled from the top down, as opposed to a complex soup of many people making many decisions. We already know how agile methods work to solve these issues by elevating and sharing work in short feedback loops to allow for more informed decision-making, which in turn helps us identify problems quickly, increase effectiveness, accelerate the pace of delivery, and cut off those compounding problems before they get out of hand. The processes, systems, and relationships that assure the work should do the same.

So yes, we need governance. Specifically, we need governance that allows for real-time clarity and the dynamic and easily accessible provision of system-based information. We need faster feedback on risk and compliance concerns. We need controls that match the way we work instead of adjusting the way we work to match the controls. Finally, we need to change the conversation around risk and governance so we can support the expansion of agile ways of working, instead of constraining agility through inappropriate and ineffective governance.

4

The Changing Face of Organizations

Environments shape organizations, and organizations in turn shape their environments by their actions and reactions. Change is one of the only constants, and only seems to ever accelerate (especially in VUCA times). In these situations, before making major changes, it's vital to identify why the change is happening, where the pressure is coming from, and what the ultimate outcome of the change should be. So be purposively considerate of the emerging challenge or opportunity to shape a customer need.

We don't stop often enough to ask ourselves critical questions, like: Why is the change happening? What signals are we receiving (and based upon what data?) that something new is happening that requires a response? It's important to clarify that VUCA comes wearing many faces and is often hard to recognize. Our first instinct when things get chaotic, volatile, uncertain, or ambiguous is to look outside our own organization, to world markets, international politics and economics, or shifting customer needs. Why not? Nobody likes admitting that their own house is in disarray. This is why, even in this age of abundant data and information, many organizations still don't turn the mirror on themselves and observe with a critical eye. However, the truth is that VUCA is both extrinsic and intrinsic.

Given that our organizations are reflections of the world outside our doors (or Zoom screens), it's safe to say that the greater the VUCA outside, the faster VUCA will grow on the inside. When nobody understands what the market wants or why existing products aren't meeting customer needs, uncertainty will grow inside teams. We resort to trying to guess the customer's need, which is often to our detriment. Communications may become chaotic. Top-down leadership may calm moods, but in many cases, it only increases volatility, and so on and so on.

We've seen this play out many times before, and the results are disastrous. For example, let's look at Blockbuster and Kodak: two major organizations brought down not through a single poor decision but through a combination of internal and external VUCA, and a reluctance to understand or adapt to the market. Blockbuster Video is often cited as having collapsed after turning down an offer to buy a budding Netflix. This is, of course, only part of the story. Netflix wasn't a sure bet at the time, and Blockbuster launched a rival service called Total Access in 2007 that boosted subscriber numbers while Netflix was busy losing its customer base. However, Blockbuster still didn't understand what customers really wanted. Punitive and predatory late fees, coupled with internal VUCA and the ousting of a customer-centric CEO in favor of a team focused on squeezing profits by increasing the cost of Total Access, meant Blockbuster was left in the dust.

Likewise with Kodak, who are often held up as the purest example of a company failing to adapt to new market conditions. In fact, we remember some meetings out at the Kodak Factory in Preston, Melbourne, while they still had it, talking about how to better adapt to digital change. Some believe that Kodak refused to pivot from film cameras to digital. As always, the truth is more complicated.

On paper, Kodak did everything right. Their teams developed the world's first digital camera and invested billions in prototyping consumer-friendly versions. They even purchased Ofoto, a photo sharing website, ten years prior to the launch of Instagram.

However, each of these moves came a little too late, and instead of listening to the customer and embracing online photo sharing, Kodak used Ofoto to promote their core business: expensive photo printing. All these factors combined saw Kodak stumble during a period of VUCA and fail to transition into the next normal. The power of the incumbent business model, and its sway over an organization's systems, processes, and therefore control mechanisms, is strong[30].

As such, organizational change is often a response to both internal and external factors. The result is that the amount of demand for change exceeds (by a wide margin) our capacity to execute it. It's not uncommon for a company to have, at any one time, multiple strategies in play to help them transition from one type of organization to another. They may even have several strategies running in tandem across different areas of the business, which leads to internal competition. The problem we've seen is that these strategies have only tenuous links to an overall organizational ambition, and don't align at all as part of any grand plan, and lead to competing KPIs where the organization is trying to retain its current business and reward it, whilst building the new. This leads to huge and growing backlogs of change as organizations struggle to identify, prioritize, and execute these plans. Worse still, by the time the solution has been rolled out, the problem has metamorphosed entirely.

When the required speed of change (an extrinsic factor) exceeds the internal capacity to change, intrinsic VUCA increases once again. This makes VUCA an exponential, accelerating force: when a company is in disarray because they're pouring all their change resources into catching up to outdated market trends,

---

[30] Anthony, S. D. (2017, April 24). Kodak's Downfall Wasn't About Technology. Harvard Business Review. https://hbr.org/2016/07/kodaks-downfall-wasnt-about-technology

customers will feel their expectations aren't being met, leading to further customer divestment, leading to more VUCA. This is the perennial self-fulfilling prophecy.

To combat this, many organizations will enter what they call a transformational state, where they profess to engage in a reinvention/transformation. What we see instead, is that they're more often becoming transitional: helping a small number of teams or departments become more agile in order to meet a specific need without the frameworks required to support long-term, whole of organization agile thinking and governance. The result is a bottleneck where a semi-effective team using agile ways of working is unable to force their products through the roadblocks thrown up by larger, more traditional systems. We see this as organizational antibodies emerging to crush a virus—without realizing, of course, that the virus they're destroying is the first step in a necessary evolution.

It's also common to see organizations do something akin to performative agile: moving people between teams, changing titles, relabeling roles, etc, but without taking any of the necessary steps to change the underlying system or structure. Even performative agile can have positive effects, and it's great to see organizations showing ambition when it comes to making positive change. Over time though, the system usually reasserts itself and the labels fall off.

Nothing changes, and VUCA stays unaddressed.

Some blame internal culture for this. You're probably familiar with the phrase, "culture eats strategy for breakfast". [31] It might be more accurate to say *the Operating Model* eats strategy for breakfast. It's rarely culture holding back change, but the fundamental ways in which the organization is built to operate and solve the known

---

[31] Peter Drucker, 2006

and current customer problem. Not the new and emergent customer opportunity.

In the market, specifically around agile transformations, you may have been witness to or read about organizations making large-scale change journeys. Retaining an existing structure is often the reason why localized moves to Tribes, Agile Release Trains or Value Streams aren't having the intended effects. Along with the principle or philosophy that designing a new Operating Model and expecting to retain your existing structure will bring success.

Ambition is easy. Breaking the established philosophies, principles, and culturally ingrained ways of working is hard. You can do it incrementally and piecemeal and we call this fractal branching; when change begins with a core pillar and then branches out over time into smaller and smaller changes. However, we often don't set the correct core pillars. We begin with simple agile concepts like Product Owners and Scrum instead of examining structure and Operating Model.

Thankfully, we're seeing the tide begin to turn. Failed transformations are common enough. The latest statistic we saw was that around 70% of transformations fail[32] to meet their core outcomes. The importance of beginning with structural change is becoming inescapable. We've also learned about the many intrinsic layers change needs to ensure success, and how important it is to synchronize them if we want to achieve any level of lasting outcomes.

So, if change is constant and VUCA is ever-present, why are we seeing so much organizational change happening in such a short space of time? You can probably guess.

---

[32] McKinsey and Company; Why do Most Transformations Fail?: July 10th, 2019; https://www.mckinsey.com/capabilities/transformation/our-insights/perspectives-on-transformation

COVID-19 and the Move to Remote

The ongoing COVID-19 pandemic is the most recent, largest, and most obvious factor in the acceleration of organizational change. It's the primary cause of global VUCA, the growth in digitality, and the ubiquity of remote working. Want to run a business in these trying times? Change, or collapse.

We *have* changed! There isn't an organization on earth that hasn't adapted itself to fit the new shape of the past three years, and the largest (and most enduring) of all those changes is the move to remote working.

Remote work isn't a new concept. In fact, the phrase "telecommuting" was coined by Jack Nilles in his 1976 book, *The Telecommunications-transportation tradeoff: options for tomorrow*[33]. IBM was already experimenting with what they called "work from home" in that period, with 2,000 employees working from home by 1983. To be fair, IBM had easier access to home PCs and terminal emulators at that time than the average Joe. However, the concept had been proven, and by 2006 over four million Americans were working from home.

As a result, much of the infrastructure that saved our collective bacon in 2020 was already in place. Zoom was already eight years old, and workers had been cursing Microsoft Teams since 2017. Webcams and fiber-to-the-home were standard, and you'd be hard-pressed to find an employee in 2019 who didn't have a passing familiarity with remote work/coworking methods and standards.

Even so, the events of early 2020 forced us to go remote, fast, and on a scale never previously considered. We did it! We collaborated, broke established norms, made the brittle parts of our companies more flexible, and performed the largest (and fastest)

---

[33] Nilles, J.M. (1976). *The Telecommunications-transportation Tradeoff*. Krieger Publishing Company.

collective shift in ways of working the world has ever seen. It was like the world of knowledge work, across every country across the globe, had acted as an almost single consciousness and achieved change virtually overnight. Even Microsoft Teams has evolved for the better.

We also witnessed a mass "radical repurposing"—a drive for organizations to take existing tools, strategies, concepts, methods or frameworks and adapt them for use in an entirely new domain. David Snowden may dub this type of event an exaptive moment[34], when stresses in the environment force a radical change in how systems are used, creating new mental pathways, and offering new possibilities. This defines remote work: as a whole, workforces operating out of the home was not a new concept in 2020. It was the sudden necessity for remote work that forced many organizations to take existing tools and methodologies and stitch them together into functioning systems. Yes, much of the infrastructure required for the remote working revolution already existed. The rest was cobbled-together, duct-taped, jerry-rigged, until we got it working the way we needed it to. These experiments resulted in all-new technologies that integrate those older technologies and processes into single, streamlined systems of work.

The shift to remote work was smoother for some organizations than others. It quickly became apparent throughout 2020 that the key when moving to remote work is that the right tooling and processes be instituted from the very beginning, in order to give everyone a solid connection to the strategy. The visibility provided by work traceability systems (which make the connection between work streams, initiatives, work items, etc.) allow everyone to see the

---

[34] Snowden, D., Greenberg, R. and Boudewijn Bertsch (2021). *Cynefin® weaving sense-making into the fabric of our world.* Singapore: Cognitive Edge - The Cynefin Co.

threads between the work on their desk and the broader strategy and goals in play. These tools make the system visible and tangible.

In addition to this, executives need to know exactly what they want before they ask for it. Because whatever they ask for, they're going to get. And once they start getting it, it won't be simple to have their teams change direction. Momentum is difficult to alter on the fly, so ensuring the strategy is both correct and well communicated is vital. Reprioritisation has a cost.

This is doubly important when discussing internal strategies, which sometimes conflict. A larger strategy, once propagated down through federated departments, teams and silos, can take on new and strange forms which create friction, if not outright competition. Friction[35] is a well-known concept in the military sphere—Carl von Clausewitz coined the term to describe the many small, surprising things that happen in wartime that upset perfect plans and make executing even the simplest strategy difficult. Stephen Bungay observed the same thing occurring in business environments, where human beings with independent wills were all trying to achieve a collective purpose in a fast-changing, complex, unpredictable environment[36]. Friction is a natural occurrence when every layer of the organization is articulating a broader strategy in a different way. Not to mention that the further down you go, the more difficult it becomes to clearly link these strategies back to the original, global vision. Remote work, and the increase in communication distance, exacerbates this.

Those organizations that knew what they wanted, that did get the right tools and processes into the right hands, and did maintain visibility, had a much better chance of surviving the remote-work transition. They've also provided us with new insights over the past

[35] *Carl Von Clausewitz: ON WAR. Book 1, Chapter 7, n.d*
[36] Bungay, S. (2012). *The art of action: how leaders close the gaps between plans, actions and results.* London: Nicholas Brealey.

years into the effects of remote work on their people, processes, and technology. Professor Nick Bloom[37] at Stanford has done the hard work of collecting and crunching the data. His conclusion: work from home has begun to stabilize across many industries at an average of around three days per week. Organizations that can't match that will experience a flight risk and lose experienced employees to more flexible companies. Who can argue with an average of 770 fewer hours spent commuting every year? Organizations believing that remote work equals lost productivity are misinformed: many employees spend the time regained from the morning commute either preparing for or actively working, meaning that most organizations have experienced steady or improved productivity. Those who have seen clear losses in productivity have more fundamental problems to solve than where or when the work gets done.

In fact, in one organization that performed productivity assessments during 2020, post the core move to work from home, found that developer metrics had improved by 20-25% as a result of remote working. Workers were becoming more efficient without leaders needing to look over their shoulders, which led to a corresponding improvement in trust and work/life balance. This raises the question: would leaders have trusted their teams enough to institute a change like this if the pandemic hadn't made it necessary? How many other positive changes have we missed out on because we haven't been forced to take a crisis-inspired leap-of-faith?

Secondary impacts of the shift to remote work are harder to sort into baskets of good versus bad. Here in Australia, where we live, inner-city property prices (especially commercial property) are cooling or even falling, contrasted by a boom in suburban or

---

[37] https://nbloom.people.stanford.edu/

regional property. Renewed interest in Australia's satellite cities is generally good for everyone, but few are happy that the formerly bustling centers of Melbourne, Sydney, and Canberra have been hollowed out by the move to remote work. Across the world, this has become evident, with London, Dallas, New York, San Francisco, and Boston for example, experiencing the same effects as shown in the McKinsey study, "Empty Spaces and Hybrid Places"[38].

So, good news! We now know that, when faced with an immovable object (like a global pandemic), we can upend so-called fixed structures and find a way to thrive in uncertain times. The majority of the knowledge-work industry—hundreds of millions of people—managed to transform overnight. A crisis emerged, and the industry responded. So, why do so many organizations continue to make flimsy excuses when faced with further change? "It's too complicated! We don't have the resources! Our culture can't sustain it!" How can we build and strengthen that response mechanism when there isn't a crisis forcing our hand?

Let's explore this question using a recent client of ours, a telecommunications provider. We were assisting with a large-scale ways-of-working transformation and our first exercises were to help everyone better understand impediments to change, and how they could deal with change now and in the future, so as to better set the stage for the upcoming transformation. The response was universal: *In a crisis, we're good! Why? Because our ways of working change to suit the situation. We have a different style of leadership: direct and controlling. We make immediate decisions and have a clear goal, which is to get*

---

[38] Mischke, J., Luby, R., Vickery, B., Woetzel, J., White, O., Sanghvi, A., Rhee, J., Fu, A., Palter, R., Dua, A., & Smit, S. (2023, July 13). *Empty spaces and hybrid places: The pandemic’s lasting impact on real estate.* McKinsey & Company. https://www.mckinsey.com/mgi/our-research/empty-spaces-and-hybrid-places

ourselves out of chaos.

In short, a crisis is well-defined, and many organizations have protocols in place that dictate how they respond to a crisis. Everyone knows their role, so the response is a whole-organization effort. However, the effectiveness of this organization's response to a crisis sheds light on why other organizations struggle to respond when they *aren't* in crisis mode. A lack of strong, direct leadership, a lack of protocols, and a fog surrounding who should be responding to what (and why their response matters, or how their work is related to the strategy). The decomposition of information and strategy simply isn't present.

This observation broadly holds true across many global industries: organizational governance hasn't changed to match the shift in ways of working, nor done enough work to evolve its processes, trust mechanisms, or speed of digitalization. In fact, even those organizations that loosened their governance mechanisms to enable more efficient remote work are now back to pulling on the reins. They're happy to keep the increases in productivity; however, they still want to address every small misstep with controls piled atop controls piled atop more controls.

We've seen this first-hand in our work with a Global Organization, where advice given during a portfolio review was, "We have a few projects that are at risk, but we still feel we're on track to complete all the planned initiatives before the end of the year." Only two weeks later, it became clear that few of those initiatives would hit their targets. In the space of a fortnight, we'd gone from a systems-view where everything was good and green, to an all-hands-to-battle-stations situation where everything was red.

How could everything have gone wrong so quickly?

The truth is, nothing had changed in those two weeks. The problem was that layers of governance had become so opaque that nobody in the portfolio review group had true visibility into what was happening at the ground level. Roles and responsibilities had become so diffuse that nobody knew what they were responsible for, and nobody owned or truly invested themselves in their projects. In short, so much governance had been added over the preceding twelve months that nobody really understood who owned or controlled projects.

Finding out why these projects had gone from green to red in such a short space of time was only half the challenge. The other half was fixing the problem. The traditional answer would be to identify gaps and add controls like weekly status checks to ensure this situation couldn't repeat. We disagreed—the answer was to take bad governance away and remove controls, thus forcing people to take greater responsibility, plug information gaps of their own volition, and approach problems from a more agile mindset.

This returns us to our original proposition: Agile Governance isn't about squeezing more governance into your agility. We want to put more agility into your existing governance. Sometimes, that means reframing certain processes and mindsets. Other times, it means removing those processes entirely.

The New Normal VS the Next Normal

When discussing the move to remote work and all it entails, people love invoking the "new normal," implying a clean delineation between one state of working and another. Others will point to the "next normal," implying a constant, never-ending stream of changes without pause for breath.

Reality, as always, lies somewhere in the middle. Change is a constant yet some aspects of how we live and work have already stabilized post-lockdown, and will remain stable for some time to come. For example, the fact that a large proportion of the workforce have adjusted to remote work and are unlikely to give it up entirely. On the other hand, changes in governance required to enable and sustain these new models will be ongoing for the foreseeable future. Inside and surrounding every "new normal" are a series of "next normals", and these interlocking changes have created a shift in what we mean by the word "transformation".

Transformation should not be viewed as an event, but a capability. The accelerating occurrence of VUCA events means that strategy needs to change increasingly often in response to exaptive events, and structure needs to be flexible enough to accommodate and deliver upon that change. In many ways, the pandemic has functioned not just as a test of how well organizations responded to a switch to remote work, but also as a test of their capabilities to continually transform throughout successive waves of economic, technological, and social upheaval. Those who were able to adjust to the new normal survived for a while... However, only the organizations who were able to adjust to the new realities of 2020 while staying on their toes and preparing for the next wave of change, and the next, and the next, were able to thrive.

The question now is: as Covid-19 becomes increasingly viewed by the public as a common, endemic illness (whether for good or ill), and the world transitions into a permanent state of hybrid remote work, will organizations retain and feed the transformational capabilities they've built since 2020? Will they grab hold of their achievements and look for ways to scale them? Or will they let that skill evaporate and, once again, see their systems of work decay and deprecate over time? Will they then outsource the problem to their consultancies when the next crisis hits?

For some organizations, that depends on whether they feel we're sitting in a semi-stable "new normal" or whether we have one foot in and one foot out of the "next normal". The difference often depends on whether those organizations feel they can predict the next great VUCA event, the next game-changer for our industries.

Is it possible? Ask ten futurists and you'll likely get ten dissenting opinions. It's fair to say that future pandemics (either fresh variants of COVID-19 or something altogether new), the roll-on effects of international conflict (which always cause ripples beyond our ability to forecast), and the normalization of AI via deep-learning, Generative Pre-trained Transformer (GPT) models, will all feature in future conversations about the next-normal. It's likely that the speed of change will continue to increase. Customer needs and demands will be increasingly complex. Adaptivity will no longer be a capability to develop only in the event of change.

All evidence suggests that the challenges faced by traditionally governed organizations will only grow over the coming years. Our processes always begin at the same point: an analysis of the current obstacle under the assumption that we already broadly know both the problem and the solution. In a VUCA world, you don't *really* know the problem. To quote Donald Rumsfeld, Former United States Secretary of Defense, VUCA problems are "the Unknown Unknowns"[39], and the solution is orders of magnitude more complex than whatever you have pre-prepared in your toolbox. Big governance is fantastic at operating in an environment with known problems, constraints, and processes. It collapses as soon as you enter the fog of complexity and uncertainty, and you need to move forward with imperfect information.

Many people believe "doing agile" will prepare them for the next normal, as if agile is a verb, a set of exercises to accomplish along the road to success. Let's dump that notion right now. Agile is not a verb. Agile is a collection of philosophies, mindsets, and

---

[39] Donald Rumsfeld. (n.d.). Oxford
Reference. https://doi.org/10.1093/acref/9780191843730.013.q-oro-ed5-00008992

imperatives that help us navigate through the gray of VUCA. Agile is not a single process, but agility is an outcome. An organization that has inherent agility is able to quickly and efficiently deploy the various tools and processes that make up what many people think of as agile. It is, however, just as important to have the agility in hand to take those processes away, reinvent them, or create something altogether new. Aiming for Minimum Viable Everything is still the done thing, as our friends from TQM and the Lean movement will often remind us—as we so often find, what's new is sometimes just something that's been rediscovered. None of that is possible if the underlying governance isn't in place to allow for that agility.

Hence the need for a remote ready Agile Governance frame of reference, that is both suited for our current "new normal" while remaining ready for the next. **Agile Governance** is built upon four key concepts: Sensible Transparency, Conductive Leadership, Patterns of Work, and Data-Driven Reasoning. It enables the power of autonomous teams to achieve high performance, if they operate in a remote setting without the need for colocation. The purpose of these four stanchions is to build a culture of distributed governance throughout the organization, which in turn distributes a sense of responsibility and ownership.

Alongside these four stanchions is a fifth, equally crucial stanchion: Humanity, the cornerstone. People are not resources, and they are not interchangeable bodies on a factory floor. All agilists know the human element. In fact, agile was founded on re-embedding humans into technology work. However, we've observed that this element needs to be re-found and established in concrete as a part of Agile Governance.

These five stanchions are not new to the world of agile ways of working. Sensible Transparency has always been considered key to enabling the flow of work, and conductive leadership rather than top-down leadership is a tried-and-tested component in helping people contribute fully and enthusiastically. Patterns of Work is a complex topic, however, and refers largely to how we proscribe the work. Finally, data is crucial for Data-Driven Reasoning when the work is happening in the office, remotely, or the hybrid in between. All of these combine to enable greater layers of integrity and trust, which allows us to apply agile values and principles to Agile Governance in the human context.

Sharing the strategic intent allows people the flexibility to decide where, how, when, and what they need to do to achieve the common objective. This is definitely not a new observation and can be found in many worthy tomes such as *Team of Teams*[40], the *Art of Action*[41], and so forth.

Given that hybrid and remote work environments are here to stay, at least for the foreseeable future, it's our belief that a shift to Agile Governance is non-optional. The benefits are indisputable: reduced traffic, greener outcomes, improved productivity, cost savings from an organizational and individual perspective, etc. Most people are enjoying better work-life balances, and that reflects on the quality of their work, and overall job satisfaction.

In an April 2020 survey, Gartner found that three-quarters of CFOs planned to increase the number of employees working remotely on a permanent basis. Suresh Kumar, Walmart Global CTO, stated: "We believe the way of working in the future, particularly in tech, will be fundamentally different than it was before. We believe it will be one in which working virtually will be the new normal, at least for most of the work we lead."

If you want to maximize the outcomes of your remote and hybrid work, you need to think of the entire organization through

---

[40] McChrystal, S.A. (2015). *Team of teams: the power of small groups in a fragmented world.* London: Portfolio.
[41] Bungay, S. (2011). *The Art of Action.* Nicholas Brealey.

the lens of Agile Governance. To do this, we need to put people back at the heart of governance and put humanity at the heart of our technology.

For that, you need to understand the five stanchions of Agile Governance.

5

Agile Governance
and the Five Stanchions

Let's recap, just in case you skipped the first few chapters to get to the juicy parts.

Governance is a broad term for the entire system through which an organization operates, as well as the processes, mechanisms, and systems traditionally used as ubiquitous mechanisms to keep people accountable for their work and outcomes. This encompasses fields like ethics, risk management, funding, and compliance amongst others.

Traditional governance operates through measures and controls. Even in purportedly agile organizations, teams are kept accountable through metrics, audits, and top-down bureaucracy. The result is a system at war with itself that can never achieve true agility.

Agile Governance takes the rules that evolved in a traditional governance ecosystem, uses them as a chrysalis for change, and emerges from them in order to enable integrity, transparency, and trust throughout a system of work. When organizations adopt new operating models with the goal of enabling agility, they need to ensure their governance is agile as well.

Agile Governance can't be definitively classified as either a framework or a process. It is an intention, a series of questions to be asked and insights to be gained, a frame of reference. It is a reflection upon the ways in which you work and the ways in which you wish you were working. It gives you new lenses, fresh eyes, but *you* must build the structure yourself in a way that fits your organization. There is nothing unique or novel about the idea of injecting agility into the way we govern—we have seen the successful adoption of these questions, intentions and philosophies in many industries and environments over the centuries. That said, we have refined the methods by which you can work through those questions, and craft the next directional actions that will take you closer to an Agile Governance system. We know it works because we've been living it for years. Now we're sharing it with you.

Before we explore the primary components of Agile Governance, it'll be useful to jump back in time and show you how and why we developed our thinking and structure. It was late 2019, and we'd already been working with a number of organizations over many years, helping them better understand their own governance and how it could be honed in service of better agile outcomes. We gave organizations fresh perspectives and helped them take a system-wide look at how they could strengthen their strategy and continue to deliver to their customers in an ever-changing world. Throughout these engagements, patterns were emerging as to what enabled good governance (and conversely, what was lacking in organizations struggling with their governance) on the change journey to be an agile organization. Around the same time, one of our contacts invited us to review a governance construct that had been set up in their business.

We decided that we needed a mechanism in place to facilitate that review and sat down to crystallize our findings and theories into what we hoped would be a simple model (and it was, in the end, though distilling complexity into approachability is no easy task). We've learned that one of the most challenging things in the world is to take a complex idea and make it simple to understand without oversimplifying it. There is a quote often attributed to Albert Einstein that fits this learning: "that all physical theories, their mathematical expressions apart ought, to lend themselves to so simple a description that even a child could understand them."[42]

We already had a wealth of information at hand on how concepts such as transparency, leadership, ways of working, and information flow impacted good governance. However, the questions were where things got interesting.

We started asking: How do these concepts intersect and influence one another? What links needed to be drawn, and which should be discarded? How could organizations self-reflect, gather the necessary data, and create insights in the service of positive change? How could we, taking a system view, use these ideas in a way that converged and transformed all our collected information into a useful, applicable tool?

Instead of starting from zero, we used the Heart of Agile as the foundation and fundamental premise which allowed us to crystallize our ideas.

What is the Heart of Agile?

To understand the stanchions of Agile Governance, and how we have evolved them, a quick synopsis of the Heart of Agile is in order. Formulated by Agile Manifesto co-author Dr. Alistair Cockburn, the Heart of Agile is a fresh approach to agile that eliminates two decades of (arguably) unnecessary complications and ornamentations and gets to the core outcome. In fact, Alistair would argue it's not fresh; it's a re-simplification. It asks: What do you really want to achieve by adopting agility? The answer is to change the world for the better, if only a little. How can you

---

[42] Ronald William Clark (2007) "Einstein: The Life and Times"; William Morrow & Company

accomplish this? With four key imperatives that stand independent of any agile toolset or process and allow you to strip away the theater and noise and get back to the basics. They are:

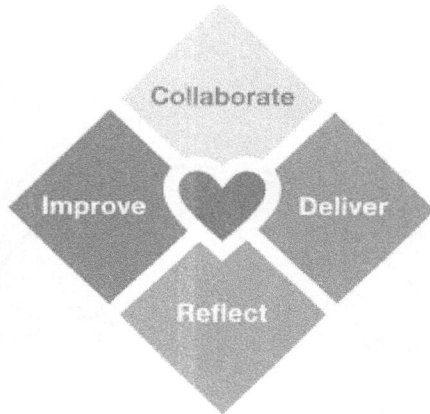

43

- *Collaborate (closely with others to generate and develop better starting ideas. Communicate often to smooth transitions);*
- *Deliver (small probes initially to learn how the world really works. Expand deliveries as you learn to predict and influence outcomes);*
- *Reflect (periodically, along the way. Think about what you've learned in your collaboration and from your deliveries); and*
- *Improve (the direction of your ideas, their technical implementation, and your internal processes).*

The key to agility, and how we use it across governance, is to master the basics. Both of us are long term proponents of Martial Arts, a never-ending journey striving for perfection. Its foundation, the root of karate, is Mastering the Basics—the Heart of Agile

---

43 Drawn from the Heart of Agile, Dr Alistair Cockburn: https://heartofagile.com/

nudges us back to that core concept. In fact, one of Alistair's other core philosophies, which he teaches in his advanced agile masterclasses, is also drawn from martial arts and supports this underpinning: the just master the basics mantra. Shu, Ha, Ri, Kokoro[44].

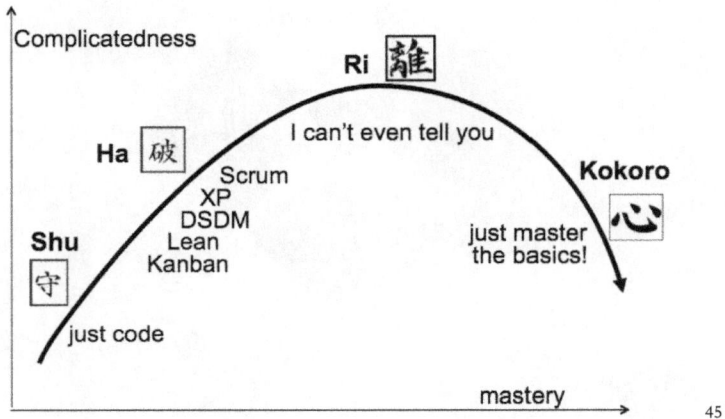

- **Shu:** This is the learning stage, where you basically just follow the rules. Think of the time when perhaps you've been to boxing classes or karate dojos for the first time and the Sensei or instructors are training their students: they expect you to just follow and learn. You follow the teaching without understanding the concept. You follow the rules.

- **Ha:** This is the stage where a student starts to branch out. Theories and concepts are starting to come into practice. Perhaps you're moving to learn from other teachers. You are actually breaking the rules.

[44] Credit: https://www.acronymat.com/2021/04/13/shu-ha-ri-kokoro/
[45] Drawn from the Heart of Agile, Dr Alistair Cockburn: https://heartofagile.com/

- **Ri:** This is where learning from others directly ends. You are the master; you are creating your own practices and passing them on to others. You are creating the rules.

- **Kokoro:** This is the spirit, the center, and the heart of things. You return to radical simplicity, and it fundamentally becomes just mastering the basics. You are returning to the core of learning, coming full circle.

If you're a long-term agilist, then you'll already recognize how these four words align with agile thinking and how you start with learning the basic practices. If you're not, we bet you can still see how these basic imperatives can drive any project, process, or community along the road to improvement.

When we began building the stanchions of Agile Governance, we wanted them to exist independently of commonly used agile ways of working. Will Kanban and Scrum still exist in their current forms in five, ten, or twenty years? It's impossible to predict. Concepts, however, like collaboration and reflection, are eternal.

Next Steps

With the Heart of Agile as our foundation, we then placed ourselves in the shoes of this organization and asked, what do you need? Our ideas evolved as we examined the why behind each need. We also knew we needed to make this model compelling. It needed to be not just a series of steps or a bundle of tools, but a story that could create investment, self-reflection, and demonstrate a relatable progression pathway. It needed to be actionable, directional, and valuable—and as a result, acceptable to the executive leadership group who commissioned the work and to whom we were providing guidance. Often you see consultant-created models that offer to solve the business problem but don't resonate with an executive team, and as a result don't gain traction. Vice versa, you also often see stories that the executive group readily align to yet fail the execution test.

We knocked our heads together until we had a working model based around what we thought were the most pivotal stanchions of Agile Governance. By presenting our review to the leadership team through the lens of those stanchions, we were able to create a level of understanding and investment we'd not quite achieved previously. They were used to construct projects focused on project management office (PMO), project governance, funding, ongoing work, etc. To their credit, they were well-versed in how agility could influence the outcomes of projects and customer satisfaction, with at least one of their large-scale digital transformations adopting elements of agile in its operating model.

By contrast, the stanchions allowed the leadership team to understand, for the first time, how (for example) specifically improving their transparency would have flow-on effects across the entire system. They were able to ask: What are we doing to generate transparency, and how do we share that information? What mechanisms are in place to maintain transparency? How do we plan for and collaborate on transparency? What are cadences and sequences of that planning? How do we visualize the flow of work, and radiate that information throughout the organization?

This leadership team was able to make big, positive changes as a result of our working model. We were excited, but we needed more data.

Over time, we have observed large amounts of governance. Expensive governance. Big governance that involved lots of people across many portfolios, programs, and projects. From billions in annual investment to millions annually and many in between. However, was it *good* governance? Was it governance aimed at solving the right problems? Did it even *know* the right problems? These were trickier questions. We continued consulting and helped a lot of businesses institute a lot of changes. We directly lobbied leadership to increase informational transparency, to be more directional in their decisions, to limit the work they were taking into the system, and so on. As we will go into detail with this particular stanchion, transparency can often be a double-edged sword that comes at a cost.

Many of the ideas we were proposing were not particularly radical. What *was* new and exciting for our clients and colleagues, was the holistic combination of these ideas into a frame of reference that affected the governance of the system *as a whole*. There were already many schools of thought on how to spread agility horizontally throughout an organization, and a few explored how to move agility through the layers. However, the idea of a single, unified method that did both sparked incredible amounts of interest that we did not expect.

All the while, we evolved our ideas. Our collection of stanchions became more focused over time, but it soon became clear that something was missing.

Our mistake was a common one. We intertwined processes and the people behind them to such an extent that the people became lost. We decided to add one final, crucial stanchion, which focused on giving the people at the heart of any system the spotlight they deserved.

It worked. The missing piece did more than fill in a gap—it elevated the entire model. We took opportunities to incorporate these ideas into other engagements. When the pandemic first hit in early 2020 and there was an exaptive moment where it seemed the entire world would move to working from home, we modified the model for the remote context. We then codified this with the Remote Agility Framework (we will explain this framework and our work on it further on in the book), as well as fresh consultancy opportunities. We tested our model in the field. We reflected. We refined it. And we continue to reflect and refine, even in the process of writing this book.

So, we come to the stanchions themselves.

The Five Stanchions of Agile Governance

The delicately curved roof of the Greek Parthenon relies on the support of sixty-nine mighty stone columns. Agile Governance manages fine with just five. These stanchions are the foundations upon which good, responsive, human-centric governance can be built. In fact, we believe these five stanchions are required for effectively governing *any* modern system of work, agile or not. You'll find most organizations are somewhat hybrid, with some agile teams, some fixed, planned waterfall teams, and some departments that blend the two. The stanchions are the connectors that combine these many methods and provide clarity, communication, and synergy. They are:

1. **Conductive Leadership;**
2. **Sensible Transparency;**
3. **Patterns of Work;**
4. **Data-Driven Reasoning; and**
5. **Humanity as the Cornerstone.**

Let's break each of those down into a bite-sized concept.

Conductive Leadership is about moving away from a mechanistic approach where people are cogs in a machine, to a humanistic approach where creativity and individualism can flourish. To be *conductive* means to operate like a conductor in an orchestra: guiding, strengthening, providing a tempo and synchronization, without directly controlling the hands of your performers. In short, if you can't change the way you lead, you can't change the way you govern.

Sensible Transparency is one of the keys to agility, namely the speed at which information flows around the organization. Without information, you can't make decisions. Without transparency of information, you can't build trust. Creating Sensible Transparency requires purposeful design which enables true collaborative connective tissues, which in turn gives you the speed and flow required for success.

Patterns of Work is the question of how we work, how we organize, and how we complete work. This encompasses processes and tools, as well as the mindsets we employ, and the systems that support and enable those mindsets. Whether it's continuous delivery, project-based thinking, charts, plans, compliance methodologies, and so on, we need to ensure our patterns of work are designed with the intention of optimizing productivity, maximizing learning, and evolving for continuous improvement. Who knows best when it comes to execution? The people doing the work: the teams and the people on the ground. Who knows best when it comes to what we need? Leaders, and what we need the teams to align to. How do we meet in the middle?

Data-Driven Reasoning is about what we measure, how we measure it, and how we use that information to make decisions. You're probably familiar with the classic metrics: time, cost, scope, and quality. What about customer satisfaction or team happiness? Are these truly the measures we need to succeed in a VUCA world? What about lead time, cycle time, and flow efficiency? And once we've decided on what data we need, how can we gather and understand it fast enough to keep up with the pace of change?

Finally, let's think of Humanity as the Cornerstone to good Agile Governance. This means putting people in the work instead of bringing work to the people. It means making workers the true custodians of good governance. A scaling down of mechanistic controls, and a maturation of trust and ownership.

These five stanchions don't just illuminate what can be added to an organization in order to improve governance. They also illuminate how you can improve governance through *removing* key factors such as misalignments, roadblocks, and entrenched cultural aspects that inhibit good governance. They are not a series of rules to follow, or an inviolable bible of how to do effective governance. We want these ideas to be taken and experimented with, shaped, evolved. We want you to use them in the ways that work for you and discard whatever doesn't. Two, five, or ten years from now, the stanchions may have taken on all-new forms and contexts thanks to you, shaped to suit the emergent business ecosystems of the 21st century.

What could be more agile, after all?

In the next chapters, we'll work through each of the five stanchions one by one and get you thinking about where your organization stands in relation to these foundational concepts.

6
Stanchion #1: Conductive Leadership

Agility, by its very nature, disseminates control. The degree to which autonomy increases can vary industry by industry or team by team, however, you can generally assume that the greater the agility, the greater the level of self-determination.

Leadership doesn't always function like this. In traditional governance models, a common practice of leadership is to design and manage tightly to control in one form or another. So, it's no wonder the emergent struggle with the introduction of agility, creates a perception of taking away or lessening that control.

This can result in less-than-desirable behaviors from people who want to retain traditional models of leadership—for example, micromanagement, new controls, constant demands for metrics proving the value of agility… We mentioned previously, in fact several times, that the harder you push for change, the harder the system pushes back. Nowhere is this more apparent than in the conduct of leaders who feel agility introduces risk.

What's the solution? Get rid of leaders? Toss out middle-management?

Absolutely not. Great leaders are game changers and essential to successful agile enterprises. While hierarchy can be a dirty word in certain contexts, we also recognize that effective hierarchies are crucial to the success of many modern, agile organizations. Having clear responsibilities and accountabilities, delineations of power over/under/for/to, and iron-clad agreements on who sets the direction for the team to row in, can all work in the favor of the customer. Meanwhile, flattened hierarchical structures such as Holacracy have enabled many organizations to find success; however, they have left other organizations tangled in webs of opaque accountabilities. Holacracy is one of those things that, although it really buys into the human element with radical autonomy, has a lot in common with communism. Looks great on paper but is often a disaster in practice.

The takeaway is that hierarchy itself is neither blessing nor curse. Context is king. An absolute verdict on leadership models isn't helpful, because no two organizations or customers are alike.

What we need is a new approach to leadership.

We call it Conductive Leadership.

Where did Conductive Leadership come from?

To understand how we came to conceptualize Conductive Leadership, we should rewind to intent-based leadership.

Intent-based leadership began when Stephen Bungay[46], historian, author, and management consultant, took mission command concepts and reframed them for the corporate context. Mission Command provides some philosophical basis for how much of the West's modern military functions and is thought to have originated and evolved in the German army in the early 1800s under the leadership of Helmut Von Moltke and termed Auftragstaktik.

From this, Bungay first coined the term "Leading with Intent", while the term "Intent-based Leadership" later followed, having been popularized by David Marquet in his book, *Turn the Ship Around*. For the purposes of this discussion, we could use the terms interchangeably.

---

[46] Bungay, S. (2011). *The Art of Action*. Hachette UK.

Intent-based leadership is a broad term, and that's great. Leadership needs to be broad. However, we saw other concepts that we wanted to slip underneath the leadership umbrella, and intent-based leadership didn't seem quite expansive enough. We needed to take intent-based leadership and unfurl it even wider than before. For example, we believed leadership should encompass the concepts of building psychological safety, employee wellbeing, building trust remotely, and even the pivotal work of Brené Brown[47] and Amy Edmondson[48], which not only centers psychological safety but also orbits concepts like team building, overcoming imposter syndrome, building genuine connections, and more.

All these things are well-known, even commonplace, in modern, effective, people-forward working environments. However, are they thought of in an integrated way? Are they considered holistically? Or are they piecemeal, a variety of quality-of-life initiatives handed off to different teams that never quite gel together or support one another?

We believe that, when you bring all these things together, they have to be combined and integrated in a systematic way. Just as the orchestra moves in concert, all vital elements of good leadership must also find a rhythm. They're reading off their own sheet music, yet also looking to the conductor to ensure they're playing in the same key, and also actively helping each other regain their tempo when someone or something inevitably misses a note. Constant rehearsal has allowed them to act as part of a collective: individual and independent, while also aligned with a greater purpose.

---

[47] Brown, B. (2018). *Dare to Lead: Brave Work. Tough Conversations. Whole Hearts.* New York: Random House.

[48] Edmondson, A.C. (2019). *The fearless organization: creating psychological safety in the workplace for learning, innovation, and growth.* Hoboken, New Jersey: John Wiley & Sons, Inc.

We also needed a metaphor that would clearly communicate our intentions and our vision of what great leaders should be able to accomplish. This had to be done while grappling with the implications of Agile—capital "A" agile, in this case—being increasingly commercialized and commoditized, broken down into a collection of saleable concepts and buzzwords. We're not objecting to the idea of organizations paying good coaches to help their teams become more agile. Rather, we have a problem with the *buzzword* being sold rather than the underlying theory and practice, stripping away the original intention and agile thinking behind it.

Take, for example, servant leadership. In a nutshell, servant leadership asks leaders to prioritize the greater good—their team, department, or organization—over themselves. They put their own objectives aside and focus on the needs of their direct reports. Sounds great. Until you dig a little deeper and consider the implications. The two terms—servant and leader—will always be in conflict. To serve is to be subservient rather than to work in concert with others. Why are you hiring leaders at all if you're not letting them lead? The concept of servant leadership is a package of ideas that sounds great at a glance and falls apart the closer you look at it. We think that what servant-leadership intends to do is something akin to intent-based leadership, but it fumbled the concept.

You don't need agilish concepts like Servant Leadership if you have strong foundations in place. Hence, we conceptualized the first of the five stanchions: Conductive Leadership.

Conductors? Like… Aluminum?

When we talk about conductors, people sometimes get tangled up in the two primary definitions: a material that transmits heat, electricity, sound, etc., versus the leader of an orchestra. In fact, the two share Latin roots: *conductus* is a carrier, while *conducere* is one who leads, brings others together, or serves. To *lead* became to *drag* or *push*, and so we arrived at the idea of conducting water through channels or power through cables. However, the idea remains the same: conductors get everyone working at the same tempo and guide their actions; however, they are ultimately in service to the larger team.

Conductive Leadership follows the same principles. It asks leaders to help teams synchronize and flow in the same direction. They don't tell people how to play their instruments (or GitHub repositories). They don't rush into the orchestra to demand metrics on strings-plucked-per-minute. They enable people to play with autonomy but stand ready to guide people towards success if they lose the beat or start playing off-key. They bring people together in service of a larger purpose. Their role is to ensure harmony, to help the teams come together to create something, a product, that an audience—a customer—can love.

At the end of a performance, the conductor takes a brief bow... before turning to bow to their orchestra, those who made the music possible.

In a business setting, Conductive Leaders focus not on elevating themselves, but upon uplifting their team and facilitating their growth and success. They build environments—in person, remote, or hybrid—that feel safe, supportive, and collaborative. They encourage connection and experimentation, while also acting as the bumpers in a bowling-rink, allowing their teams to bounce back and forth while always staying on a trajectory towards shared goals.

Shifting to a model of Conductive Leadership means a transition to a number of new modalities. Let's explore them one by one.

Leading with Intent

At its core, Intent-Based Leadership[49] is about giving those you lead the intrinsic motivation to love and succeed in their work. Create an intent for the team, the department, the business, and invest everyone with that same intent so that they're motivated and excited to hit their goals and create value for customers.

This requires leaders to push autonomy outward: to people, teams, and even other leaders. Give everyone the maximum possible ability to make important decisions, while providing clear guide rails that ensure those decisions are in alignment with the larger strategic vision. Those guide rails also let people know when a decision needs to be escalated.

Doing this requires leaders to address and understand what needs to be communicated and reported in order for teams to operate well. That may mean exploring synchronous versus asynchronous communication, increasing transparency of information, and handing back time to leaders and teams by eliminating meetings and micromanagement culture. This is especially crucial in a hybrid or remote-work environment, where information cannot be shared as easily. Conductive leaders must ensure all have the information they need to do their jobs, while creating opportunities—virtual or otherwise—for their team to connect, share, discuss, and align.

Cognizance and Responsibility

We want everyone in an organization to be aware of what's expected of them and what isn't. What they can do with their autonomy, and where the guardrails lie. What policies grant them

---

[49] As created by David Marquet. For more information, we recommend: Louis David Marquet (2015). *Turn the ship around! a true story of turning followers into leaders*. New York Portfolio Penguin New York Portfolio Penguin.

freedom and what policies need to be strictly adhered to.

This ties in with the clear flow of information that comes with Intent-Based Leadership and allows people to make important decisions without butting their heads against policies they didn't know existed. When everyone is aware of the guide rails, they can operate faster and more freely inside those bounds.

This also impacts upon the concept of trust. If we can't trust our team to take responsibility for their work—either because we don't know our teammates on a personal level, or they haven't had an opportunity to demonstrate their competence—we're headed for trouble. Humans don't always trust easily, especially if they've had difficult encounters in the past. It's harder still in a remote-work environment, where interpersonal communications are limited to text or the occasional video call. In these situations, Conductive Leaders must first allow their team members to trust them, by being transparent, reliable, and consistent in their actions, communications, and approaches. Only then will team members open up, become vulnerable, and begin to demonstrate what they're truly capable of.

Responsibility is a crucial topic to discuss in the context of Agile Governance, because it's fundamental to agility as a whole. It also sometimes is mentioned in the same breath as accountability, so let's take a moment to clarify.

An engineer is *responsible* for completing tasks. They owe this to their team, their leaders, and their customers. Nobody is going to watch over their shoulders to make sure the work is complete; it is their responsibility to complete it to the highest possible level of quality. It's important to understand that responsibility can't be *given*. It must be taken by the person in question, willingly and enthusiastically.

Accountability is concerned with what happens after the work is delivered and is concerned with taking ownership over results and outcomes. If you're *accountable* for the work, you're the one who takes the heat if the work doesn't reach expectations. Accountability for a project should generally be shouldered by one person and one person only. In other words, the leader.

A conductor is not responsible for playing the flute or plucking the harp. They trust that responsibility to the members of their orchestra. They do, however, become accountable for the overall performance of the orchestra. When one member plays a bad note or loses time, the conductor guides them back into alignment with the rest of the team. If half the orchestra is losing time... well, we have to wonder whether the conductor has set proper expectations or given their team the necessary training. If the performance is terrible, the audience won't be glaring at individual musicians. They expect the conductor to be accountable.

The lines between accountability and responsibility can be blurry. Leaders are often accountable for their teams while also being responsible for work handed to them by other leaders. It's also easy to wonder whether the differences between accountability and responsibility are purely corporate semantics. How often do you hear the word "accountable" outside the office? Is it purely a label for leadership responsibility? That's a debate bigger than this chapter.

What's important is this: people must have a sense of ownership and pride over their work. Maybe their work is software engineering. Maybe their work is teaching. Maybe their work is facilitating the work of others. Sure, we can categorize these people into little boxes marked *employees* or *leaders* or *coaches*, and we can discuss our expectations for them in terms of *accountability* or *responsibility*. So long as we ensure everyone wants to do well, wants to perform above expectations, wants to stand next to their work and say *I did this, and I own the results.*

It takes Conductive Leadership to create this environment: a place of positivity and psychological safety, where everyone has a growth mindset and a willingness to learn from failure. Without it, we very often see buck-passing, excuses, or misunderstandings when it comes to taking the blame for mistakes (but fewer misunderstandings when it's time to gather accolades for successes. Funny, that.)

A question often raised at this point: who conducts the conductor? Who ensures the leader feels safe and takes ownership over their outcomes? The obvious answer: other leaders. But that's a bit too simple. Leaders do not sit outside the environment they create. If they build an atmosphere of psychological safety for their team(s), they are also existing inside that atmosphere. If they build ownership and responsibility throughout their teams, they will find it easier to take ownership over the team's outcomes.

Create Clarity of Focus

People can't work freely and enthusiastically if the path ahead is foggy and littered with trip hazards. Leaders can help conduct their teams by clearing those impediments and providing a psychologically safe environment in which people can ask questions, make mistakes, and work their way through the fog without falling over their own feet. When we think about psychological safety, we often think about it through the lens of the Aristotelian work Google conducted in 2012 around what made their teams the most effective and efficient. After years of research with over a hundred teams, they found that understanding and influencing group norms were the keys to improving Google's teams—which norms mattered? They found it was about social sensitivity, that anyone on the team was comfortable speaking up without feeling embarrassed, punished, or blamed. That's the essence of great agile teams, and it's the role of leaders to create that space. It's essential to foster clarity of focus: a clear view of the goal, the route, the resources required, and the steps taken along the way. This is one of the hardest things to do for leaders in complex modern organizations. The amount of volatility, uncertainty, ambiguity, and complexity in our integrated world is actually growing when we think about how we currently build and deploy customer solutions using hundreds of Software as a Service (SaaS) products. Add to this the fact that we are made up of hundreds and even thousands of individuals who are nonlinear and unpredictable. The world is constantly offering endless opportunities and challenges that need to be resolved to ensure the sustainability of our company, which adds to the role and challenges for the leadership group: to be able to cut through the noise of options and opinions and make information clear so our people know what to do. How often do you find companies with competing strategies and conflicting KPIs that cause confusion? On the one hand, we don't want to over-simplify, though we do need to make information simple enough that people can make the right next decision. Clear strategies that decompose to work and allow people to make decisions to head in the right direction are critical to organizational success, and one of the fundamental roles of the leader. Conduct people toward the right goal.

This is a balancing act for leaders. Providing clear direction while also allowing each member of the team space to find their own unique path can take time. It's especially difficult when the leader is expected to be invisible: a conductive presence gently guiding people through complexities without ever actually grabbing them by the hand. Good leaders set expectations, provide the resources needed to reach those goals, and build frameworks for tracking progress… and then let their teams walk the road. As 6th Century BC philosopher Laozi[50] said, "A leader is best when people

---

[50] Lao Zi, 6-5th Century BC, Sourced from https://en.wikiquote.org/wiki/Laozi

barely know that he exists, not so good when people obey and acclaim him, worst when they despise him. Fail to honor people, they fail to honor you. But of a good leader, who talks little, when his work is done, his aims fulfilled, they will all say, 'We did this ourselves.'"

Be Flexible and Adaptable

The needs of the team are always changing. Sometimes it's the result of evolutions within the workplace. Sometimes it's due to shifts outside the office. Remote-working or hybrid-work teams may engage with the work at different hours, enjoy different holidays, observe different schedules based on cultural and religious practices, etc.

A rigid leader will force their team into a box full of checks, balances, constraints, and iron-clad expectations… and in the process, utterly crush their team. Conductive Leaders, on the other hand, must be flexible enough to change ways of working to suit the needs of the team, and adaptable enough to reshape their own assumptions and processes in order to get the best results for customers and colleagues. A good Conductive Leader is always open to exploring new approaches and technologies, and reflecting on how they can best support their team, maximize collaboration, and boost productivity in ways that suit their team's unique needs and situations.

Speaking of which…

Encourage Collaboration

This is important enough to get its own modality. Collaboration is king. Without it, 21st century teams will collapse. Sharing ideas, brainstorming, and trystorming, joining forces to work on passion

---

on 26th December 2023

projects… This is the heart of a great team. It's where people can achieve quick wins and build trust in one another. Collaboration forges lifelong bonds, stronger than anything you can create through isolated, siloed work.

Good Conductive Leaders are proactive in creating collaboration opportunities. If their team is hybrid or remote, they find online work management platforms and run virtual brainstorming sessions. If everyone is sharing an office, they do it in person. What's vital is that they don't wait for collaboration to occur spontaneously. They build instances where teamwork can flourish, and then nurture the results.

What we find, particularly in large organizations, is that collaboration doesn't come naturally, especially when you take into account the remote context in which large proportions of our people do not physically attend their place of work, and as we often like to refer to: "in remote, silos become chasms". We don't see each other enough to have the passing quick conversation, the sideways nod, the ability to grab a coffee, or even just have a chat about how things are going. There is an element of emerging data that says, if you interpret it, that the burden on leadership has grown proportionally larger with the distribution of the workforce because it becomes a role of the leader to connect not only within their team but between teams. We often see employee experience surveys that talk about great collaboration within a small team, which then diminishes or disappears as it crosses team boundaries. The ask of leadership is not only building collaboration within their team but also finding the opportunities to allow this to emerge, provide benefit, and allow decisions to be made faster and things to move forward.

A great mechanism we have used in the past to find, encourage, and enhance collaboration was created by Craig Brown— Collaboration in Eight Easy Steps. We know about this model because we asked Craig to present it. The key is starting with what you think good collaboration looks like, what makes it better, and the maturity pathway. This pathway draws on the work of Dr. Neil Preston and shows the ratio of collaborative maturity[51] starting at the bottom, where corruption lives, maturing to competition, compliance, and collaboration, and ultimately ending in an environment where co-creation thrives.

Many organizations get to compliance and cooperation, rarely to collaboration, and co-creation is still an emergent property. The leader's role is to take the organization as far up that ratio as possible to allow the organization to benefit from the diversity of its people, their ideas, their passion, and their determination.

Competency and Training

What falls underneath the umbrella of Conductive leadership is the responsibility to ensure that all those people working underneath you have a competency and that if there's a gap in their competency then you are able to enable them to succeed.

We often talk about building capabilities through upskilling. What employer doesn't want their employees to build their skillset, deliver more value to both the company and customers, and move sideways or upwards into the positions most suited to their new talents?

What we often sidestep (or sidle past, eyes averted) are the mechanisms for helping people upskill, and who will take responsibility for guiding, delivering, and verifying that growth in skills. We also don't like paying for it. It's not uncommon that, when times get tight, the first budgets we cut are for further training.

---

[51] Dr Neil Preston, Paper; May 2017; Becoming a Collaborative Leader; Psyopus.com.au;

The way we envision the concept of competency and training stems from our experiences in the military; specifically, the way the military aggressively pursues training across the rank and file. Competent militaries understand the value of a highly skilled, highly motivated force who are always looking to learn, and who (in the process of learning) understand how to pass those skills on to those who follow in their footsteps. It's a common saying in the army: train hard, fight easy. If you're not in the process of fighting, you need to be training; when the fighting begins, you won't have the opportunity to ask for a time-out and get your troops fighting fit. You need those patterns and heuristics to kick in automatically, or you'll be going home in tatters.

Yet, even as the world becomes increasingly VUCA and the fight for customers and market share approaches the doorsteps of organizations all over the world, leaders still aren't being proactive and training their employees in advance of those crises.

When leaders *do* take training seriously, the results are fantastic. As we write this, we're preparing to meet with the portfolio team of a large-scale Global Organization. They have time and resources budgeted for training, which builds competencies across a broad sweep of teams. We expect that we'll be able to check on the team the week after training and ask, what do you now know? What do you feel competent in? How can you demonstrate it? The muscle memory will be built before the crisis arrives.

That last point—asking how new skills can be demonstrated—is vital. Ensuring that your people have the right skills and competencies to do the work is an investment both in the individual and in the organization as a whole, but those skills can't just be on paper. Unless the teams also build muscle memory—the ability to leap into action without thinking and put those skills to use—then they may as well just be training manuals stored in a nearby filing cabinet. Competency and training only become useful through application. Plus, muscle memory spreads by osmosis. Skills learned by one team will, over time, translate outward through an organization (but only if you give people opportunities to demonstrate their skills in new situations and with new people surrounding them). Just as individuals can build muscle memory, so will teams and departments... We can even discuss muscle memory on an enterprise and organizational level.

Also of note, to continue our muscle-memory metaphor: when you first learn an activity, your brain's pre-motor cortex and basal ganglia light up as you actively think through and problem-solve the activity for the first, second, third... or even hundredth time. The more you demonstrate understanding through application, the more that brain activity moves into the main motor cortex and cerebellum, while the premotor cortex and basal ganglia take a rest. In other words, *thinking* shifts from the active areas of the brain into the automatic areas. We see the same in organizations: demonstrate mastery of a skill a hundred times, and even if you put it to rest for months or years, the organization will still retain that knowledge and be ready to spring into action when the time is right.

Building competencies is not limited to directly delivering work. Teams must also become competent and trained in routines such as decision-making. You can conceptualize the process behind becoming competent at decision-making with something like the Cynefin framework, which gives users a solid foundation or "sense of place" from which to view and evaluate their perceptions. When a portfolio runs on repeatable processes, the decisions commonly made within that portfolio are part of the standard operating procedure. Thus, more abstract processes such as making decisions, resolving tensions, or prioritizing WIP can be repeated, refined, evaluated, and become part of the team muscle memory.

We mentioned earlier that our experiences of competency and training have military roots. Military personnel often find themselves in chaotic situations, which corresponds with one of the four domains of the Cynefin framework. Their mission is often to move through these domains—from Chaos to Complex, then Complicated, and finally Clear—before making further life-or-death decisions (a simplification, we know—gathering enough information to move from Chaos to Complex is often, in itself, life or death).

When a squad is caught in a Chaotic situation, it needs a number of things if it's to survive. Chief among those is the aforementioned muscle memory, and the leadership required to chart a course out of the chaos. The leader decides the direction of travel, the prioritization of tasks required to survive. However, they don't hold their squad's rifles for them, or direct every bullet. They don't form a group huddle and prioritize their next steps on a Kanban board. The situation necessitates intent-based leadership: the leader will say, *I need you to accomplish X and Y and my best information indicates you should begin by heading to Z,* but after that point, the leader must trust their people to get the job done according to their training.

So, we return to our original point: the responsibility for ensuring teams have these competencies and are able to demonstrate them falls to the leaders; however, Conductive Leadership implies that the leaders then need to stand back and let the teams do the work. Leaders guide, uplift, and protect. They don't lean over their team's shoulders or snatch away their keyboards when things aren't going according to plan—that demonstrates a lack of training for both the team and the leader. Sometimes, in extreme chaos, the leader might call a pause and make sure everyone is aligned with their larger objectives. However, on the whole, there is a level of trust in the competence and clarity of the individual.

Be Empathic

The ability to place yourself within someone's frame of reference and to be open and understanding regarding their concerns, struggles, and emotional states, is essential for Conductive Leaders. We could also argue that it's essential for *everyone* to always be developing their empathy, but for the purposes of brevity, let's limit the conversation to leadership. Great leaders understand and respond to the concerns of their team members. They listen to the team's needs and work to create an open, supportive environment in which those needs can be shared and met.

This is especially crucial in a hybrid work environment, where feelings of disconnection or isolation are common. Conductive Leaders are proactive in reaching out to their team, building opportunities to share and align, and ensuring that everyone feels part of a greater, supportive whole… even if that team is spread across continents and have never met in person.

Conductive Leadership is to Serve

Conductive Leadership asks leaders to abandon mechanistic approaches that view people as cogs in a machine, and instead take a humanistic approach where everyone's individuality and creativity can flourish and guide the work.

In large scale corporate environments, we rarely directly manage all the people that are involved in the delivery of outcomes we are accountable for. We don't have any guarantee that the people have been put through a disciplined training/induction process with military rigor, and we're often managing contractors and externals from completely different cultures. Mission command is great when you have your own justice system and you can court martial your "employees", but corporate leaders don't operate in remotely similar conditions. Your primary job is not preparing for war, you're in a constant state of warfare in the marketplace and there's no penalty for treason if they jump ship to a competitor—and take your market IP with them. Yet, we still need to get results from the efforts of thousands of people, and if you think about Dunbar's number, we can hold meaningful relationships with about 150 of them. Theories such as intent based leadership work well in these domains, and can transition with principles, yet in practice can be difficult to meaningfully implement.

We understand that this is easier said than done. It asks leaders to abandon many of the things they've internalized as standard operating procedure in management school or over years of traditional middle-management. It forces them to become coaches and guides who support people's growth, and replaces preventative constraints with enabling constraints.

Most of all, it requires growth. As per Jack Welch: "Before you are a leader, success is all about growing yourself. When you become a leader, success is all about growing others." [52] Through Conductive Leadership, everyone has the opportunity to extend themselves, to nurture themselves and others, to raise up those around them.

To be a Conductive Leader is to serve, enable, and to celebrate the successes of others, and the whole.

---

[52] https://jackwelch.strayer.edu/winning/meaning-of-leadership-2/

7

Stanchion #2: Sensible Transparency

The Oxford dictionary defines agility as the ability to move quickly and easily.

Dexterously? Adaptively? With purposeful intent? These are all vital aspects of agility, absolutely. However, *quickly* is the first word, the most important word. Without speed, agility collapses. That could refer to the speed of decision-making, the speed of data gathering and processing, the speed of reactivity...

All of which relies upon Sensible Transparency.

We're all professionals here. We know how to gather information, how to process and disseminate it. We know how to sit down with colleagues and come to mutually satisfying decisions on direction.

However, we can't do those things at speed if traditional governance has boxed us in with tall, impermeable walls. Those walls may be literal and physical (the locational siloing of teams, information only being delivered face-to-face), digital (restricted networks, teams dedicated to "amending" language in internal communication), emotional (individuals feeling they can't trust one another, and therefore retaining crucial insights), inter-departmental (why would sales need to know the engineering budget?), or any other number of ways in which the flow of information is deliberately or unconsciously restricted. Why do so many organizations build these walls? Adherence to tradition? Maybe.

Often, it's not the organization but the individuals. Transparency is great, but it also invites criticism. Share an idea; get a whack because someone thinks it's stupid or it's been tried before. Share a report; get a whack because someone doesn't trust the data. Share a work product; get a whack because someone could have done it better. It's that "easy to criticize, hard to create" idea. Or, to use a food metaphor, why food critics tend to make terrible chefs. There may also be a fear that teams will lose effectiveness unless they're only delivered exactly the information required for their jobs.

This is why, without Sensible Transparency, even the most progressive agile organizations will struggle to reach their potential. We specify Sensible Transparency here because many agile teams are great at being transparent. They communicate well, share everything they know, and trust each other to get the work done. However, when we zoom out and consider governance of the system as a whole, we find obstacles everywhere.

Sometimes this is deliberate. More often it's an evolution of scarcity—when we're short on resources and time, we tend to put our heads down and focus on the work. As such, communication only moves as far as the team we're working with. Other times, a lack of transparency can be a consequence of operating models. Our functions are often optimized for strict hierarchies, so the more we share outside our departments, the less efficient we become (at least, in theory). We trust "us", but we don't trust "them". How many times do you hear of companies where people and performance scores show great team collaboration, but increasingly less when expanding the boundary? That's the funny yet sad thing about tribes and western culture—tribes often go to war with each other.

Measuring and rewarding the performance of individual silos is another obstacle to communication. When silos are competing, levels of collaboration go down. We often see whole organizations with multiple unaligned, conflicting, and competing strategies, which only serve to emphasize silos across functions. And, of course, we have the rare occasions when information scarcity is intentional. Why would somebody choose to withhold information that could benefit their team, department, or organization as a whole? Maybe it's the inescapable specter of corporate politics. Maybe it's about preservation of status or an ego-centric view that knowledge equals power, while dissemination of knowledge results in the dilution of that power. Sometimes, an individual's survival instincts can hurt those around them, draining their sense of safety and security.

Having seen the inside workings of countless companies over the years, we've come to advocate for complete Organization Transparency regardless of whether an organization is "agile" or not. Transparency of information, both good and bad, increases speed. It removes ego and enables better decision-making. It boosts trust. There's no spin, no flimflam. Just the necessary facts, available to everyone when and where they need them.

Note: we say *necessary facts*. Not everything can and should be 100% transparent. I'm sure you can name a hundred things within your team, department, or organization that shouldn't be shared openly. Esther Derby provides a great insight into this in her Cutter Journal article *Knowledge Is Bifurcated*[53], where she describes the Zone of Transparency: a concept that refers to the level of openness and honesty in an organization's communication.

This zone is the area where employees can speak freely about their opinions, experiences, and concerns without fear of retaliation. This creates an environment of trust and transparency, where individuals feel comfortable sharing their thoughts and ideas.

---

[53] https://www.cutter.com/article/knowledge-bifurcated-475956

Creating and maintaining a zone of transparency is crucial for organizations to identify and solve problems effectively, build relationships, and foster a positive culture.

Esther also describes the concept of "bifurcation of knowledge". This relates to the zone of transparency in that it recognizes the existence of two separate types of knowledge in an organization: explicit knowledge, which is shared openly and transparently, and tacit knowledge, which is not easily shared or communicated. Bifurcation of knowledge acknowledges that explicit and tacit knowledge are both essential for organizations to function effectively and efficiently. Esther argues that organizations must strive to balance explicit and tacit knowledge to achieve their goals and create a positive culture.

In short, take the time to identify what information within your organization, team, department, system, etc. is explicit and what is tacit, and find ways to ensure they're treated accordingly. If you can't be transparent with information, you can instead be transparent about what and why you're unable to share. To quote a text with significantly more pedigree than any agile text: *"And ye shall know the truth, and the truth shall make you free."*[54] Whether you're religious or not, you'll often find wisdom in the classics.

So, what does implementing Sensible Transparency actually mean? What key imperatives do companies need to consider before diving in?

Transparency is Scary

We mean it. When people not used to complete transparency are immersed in a culture where everyone shares, information is free, and collaboration is the rule, they can become intimidated.

---

[54] John 8:32. Holy Bible: Containing the Old and New Testaments: King James Version. (n.d.). New York: American Bible Society.

Why? Isn't transparency freeing? Sure, unless you make a mistake. Just as cats cover their food when they're anxious about predators, people become anxious when they may be blamed for their innocent errors. Having the ability to experiment, to raise questions or concerns, to make mistakes, and to grow in understanding, all without being punished or humiliated, is known as psychological safety. Project Aristotle—that two-year initiative launched by Google to investigate high performing teams—identified this as one of the five most crucial factors that helped teams excel.[55]

Creating psychological safety in cultures that are pathologic or blame-based generally does not encourage high performance. Instead, they encourage butt-covering. What we need to go alongside our culture of transparency is a culture of inquiry, of sharing, of interpreting failures through a lens of reflection and improvement. Only then can we make transparency exciting instead of terrifying.

Directional Decisions and Expedient Interventions = Limited Information

This is a very broad statement, and you can probably recall instances where a leader making a decisive intervention was for the ultimate betterment of the team. However, a pattern of frequent directional decisions often betrays a broken system, where mental models are rigid, information is limited to a few, and the first response to complications is, "But this is the way we've always done it." Others rely on directional decisions because they're afraid of getting caught up in endless debate. Too many cooks spoil the broth, or so they say. A single head chef saying *this is the way* is the route to success.

---

[55] https://www.nytimes.com/2016/02/28/magazine/what-google-learned-from-its-quest-to-build-the-perfect-team.html?smid=pl-share

We disagree. If collaborative decision-making is slow, it's because not everyone has enough of the relevant facts from the beginning. In today's complex world, if you wait for all the facts—or conduct extensive, up-front analysis—the problems will have changed before you get started on the solution. If mental models are rigid and the organization has always worked a certain way, maybe you need to examine all the decisions that prior projects took from start to "done" and ask whether those models are fit for purpose.

Only when data becomes transparent, ubiquitous, and accessible can decision-making become truly collaborative. More people with more information and more freedom to speak their minds means more dynamic, reactive decisions! While we can't eliminate the occasional need for an expedient intervention, true Sensible Transparency should help make decisions easier, faster, and more aligned to the organization's core mission. In fact, over time, we want to see an increase in proactive decisions and actions based on transparency of information, and less reactive firefighting.

Which leads us to:

We Must Embody our Strategic Alignment

Every organization has a mission. Whether it lives up to that mission is a different question. Sometimes, from the outside or even from inside information silos, it can appear that everyone is rowing in the same direction. Companies mail out glossy annual reports articulating the organization's North Star, or Southern Cross for those of us in the Antipodes, and all the progress they've made towards achieving it—all in line with a pre-existing plan, of course. Meanwhile, strategy may have gotten tangled behind closed doors.

It's easier to hide those situations when information isn't being shared. Much, much harder when practicing Sensible Transparency.

High transparency makes the links between vision, strategy, and execution immediately visible. It helps to expose when we're wandering off-track, and allows everyone to get aligned, fast.

Bi-Directional Flow Makes Transparency Work

By which we mean, information needs to flow both ways. Or *all* ways. Not waterfalling down on a need-to know basis, or being delivered through all-hands meetings and mind-numbing PowerPoints, or being sent up from the teams every month only to vanish into a black hole of management. We need constant, asynchronous information flow going up, down, and sideways.

It's easy to imagine this sort of information flow becoming overwhelming. Not so! Transparency means that people can access the information they need when they need it and ignore the information that isn't relevant to their goals.

How will people know what information is relevant and what isn't?

A good question. Many organizations are now dealing with an explosion of information larger than any single person or department can handle. Too many insights and too many opportunities can be just as stifling and restrictive as having too few. The need for fast progress often means moving forward with imperfect information, and then adjusting the course based upon a constant flow of relevant feedback. Handling this means organizations need to build robust systems which can provide continuous feedback and analytics, separating the wheat from the chaff. Doing so enables you to forge useful insights from reams of raw data.

It's not always easy. However, we promise you: transparency through bi-directional information flow is the easiest, fastest, and most cost-effective way to make sure everyone knows what they need to, when they need to.

Note: There's often a trade-off to this. Transparency also invites fear—fear of failure, fear of uncovering true issues that have hidden for years, and fear of status and ego being lost. We mentioned earlier that transparency is a double-edged sword. Sometimes you learn things that, in hindsight, you didn't want to know. However, to mix our metaphors, you can't put the genie back in the bottle. Instead, you must act with resolve and move forward.

With all this in hand, let's ask: who is responsible for creating Sensible Transparency? Who has the ability to open up flows of information, or to create conversations that draw people in both horizontally and vertically?

The answer: leaders and managers. While everyone in an organization is responsible for disseminating, interpreting, and collaborating, only leaders can address the larger operating models that allow for accelerated information flow. Only leaders can ensure everyone has access to what they need, when they need it. Only leaders can work to reshape existing governance in a way that supports and generates transparency. Leaders have the true power to change the system via their decision-making and behaviors. We see time and time again that although the people doing the work know what needs to change, they don't have the delegation, authority, or support to really attack systemic concerns. That's where the difference between leaders and managers is found.

Transparency is Where to Begin

If you want to make better decisions faster and accelerate the creation of value, transparency is where you begin. Start sharing information more freely; even if you're not sure the data is 100% correct, if it's enough to drive a conversion, start a dialogue, or support an action, it's worth the risk. Of course, it goes without saying that this is limited; you don't want to give away commercially sensitive material or strategy if it's not public. We don't mean sharing Personal Identifiable Information. However, we do mean information about internal performance. If someone has joined your organization, signed their employment agreement, then that's generally enough for most information to be shareable. As Dr. Alastair Cockburn once put it, *"Internal collaboration is not espionage."*

8

Stanchion #3: Patterns of Work

Look over the shoulder of any software engineer and you'll quickly get a sense of how they work: their approaches, their toolsets, the ways they track and verify completion of tasks. Zoom out a little and now watch the entire team at work. What ways of working are shared by all? What rituals and processes? How do they communicate, collaborate, celebrate? Zoom out once more, so you can see an entire department or even a small company achieving their goals. Where are the patterns emerging? What unites these people in their pursuit of excellence?

This combination of teamwork and taskwork as expressed across a wide breadth of workers—engineers or otherwise—forms what we refer to as Patterns of Work.

From a traditional governance perspective, Patterns of Work encompass all the ways in which teams, individuals, and departments plan projects, comply with processes, hold to tightly mandated delivery windows, achieve goals, and how all these concepts vary in accordance with the constraints of time, cost, and project scope. This way of thinking is fantastic if you're working in a stable ecosystem with very little change on the horizon. You can create a work package designed for a single outcome and execute it precisely. But it all falls apart when you need to create a model of continuous delivery that flexes to match changes in the environment and the needs of customers. In our modern, VUCA world, these windows of change have contracted significantly. Back in the 1990s, you had three to four years to respond to market shifts. Today? Six months, if you're lucky. How often have you seen new strategic opportunities or challenges emerge before we've managed a response to the crisis of the moment?[56]

High performing agile organizations, on the other hand, allow teams to define their own localized ways of working. They build safe spaces where teams can exchange ideas, experiment with processes, and allow individualized toolsets and approaches to flourish. This isn't to say that those teams operate without constraints. They still work beneath the umbrella of organizational structures and patterns required to ensure overarching strategic alignment. But the *how* is decided upon at the team level.

When traditional governance reigns, these safe spaces are often limited to specific teams or departments. You're all probably familiar with organizations where a handful of agile teams are highly successful in defining their own ways of working, but that permission to experiment is constrained. What could become fantastic new patterns of work across the breadth of an organization are locked down to pilot teams or artificially hobbled by middle-management compliance with a systemic bent to control.

We already know how effective these new ways of working can be in a VUCA environment. It's governance that needs to change by:

- Distributing permission for individuals and teams to discover their own, localized ways of working;
- Moving away from mandated processes and towards high-level guided intent;

---

[56] For more on this, see Thomsett, R. (2002). *Radical project management*. Upper Saddle River, Nj: Prentice Hall Ptr.

- Instead of providing teams with designed ways of working, seeking to understand and verify the question, "Have you intelligently designed for the work that needs to be done?";
- Providing guide rails to gently nudge people towards ways of working that suit their teams, goals, and customers;
- Creating environments where people feel safe to experiment with new patterns of work, and where failures are considered learning opportunities.

Easier said than done, of course. Leave teams with complete freedom to design their own patterns of work, and they may create something that's highly effective for them but clashes with the rest of the organization, hindering communication and productivity across the horizontal. Tighten the guide rails too much, and you have the opposite problem: organic patterns of work become stifled, with no way to devolve across teams and departments.

So how can we create new systems of work that allow for and encourage these high-productivity patterns of work? Or, considering that your systems of work will be highly individualized and molded to your organization in extremely specific ways, what markers or signposts should we look for in our systems of work that let us know we're on the right track?

There are four essential imperatives to encourage:

Design for Flow

If you want to get the most out of a tank of petrol, hit the highway and stay on cruise control. Similarly, if you want to create value more efficiently, make sure your teams are working steadily at an optimal rate.

We see huge inefficiencies arise when teams stop and start, stop and start, thanks to lags and delays between projects, getting stuck at bottlenecks, poor information flow, or delayed decision-making.

When knowledge workers are on the deck and the payroll, you want to keep them working. This might sound like cold economics, but it's demonstrable that passionate engineers thrive when they're working on projects that they're passionate about and in ways that allow them to express that passion. Nobody enjoys spinning their wheels, and team morale suffers as a result.

What we need is a steady, managed, and prioritized flow of work stemming from customer needs. Organizations are increasingly recognizing this need and thinking in terms of Flow, not just as a process but as a philosophy of work. To which some say: What took you so long? Toyota has been developing the Toyota Production System (TPS) and the Toyota Way for over half a century. Honda, Porsche, and most other major automotive manufacturers have followed suit. The Toyota Way, and offshoots, aren't limited to manufacturing: it has since been built upon and extended into software development and organization design thanks to the guidance of heavyweights like Don Reinertsen (Product Development Flow) and Mary & Tom Poppendieck (Lean Software Development).

A more broadly applicable adaptation of this way of thinking is The Flow System, which is an evolution of Lean Thinking. The Flow System[57] was developed as a framework by Turner, Thurlow and Rivera in 2019 to "[provide] a re-imagined system for organizations to understand complexity, embrace teamwork, and autonomous team-based leadership structures."

The Flow System resonates across a broad spectrum because of how it incorporates complexity thinking. This takes the core, successful foundations of Lean and TPS and uses them as a guiding pattern for domains that aren't linear, predictable, or deterministic.

---

[57] John R. Turner, Ph.D. Nigel Thurlow Brian "Ponch" Rivera: The Flow System Guide; Version 1.0 (November 2019) https://flowguides.org/Flow_Guide.pdf

Don't have time to dive deep into the Flow System? Don't worry. We'll explore how to design for flow in a nutshell.

The first step is to adopt Value Chains and Value Stream Mapping across the entire organization. We won't go into depth in this book about Value Stream Management and Value Stream Mapping, however, we consider them fundamental to governing any system of work or executing a transformation. Think of it as the evolution of process mapping with a customer-first lens applied to creative or knowledge work, which is often hidden work. You can't see the knowledge worker flow of activity the way you can see a factory floor.

Yes, Value Chains are now commonplace in many teams. But do these ways of thinking extend throughout the hierarchy to touch all levels of governance? Can people three or four steps removed from the work (and the customers) accurately visualize the flow of work through the system? Do knowledge workers have complete visibility into interdependencies and bottlenecks that exist outside their own teams?

Take the fundamental principles of Value Stream Mapping and expand it. Look not just at the work being done, but at how the organization functions to get value into the hands of its customers. Only then can you ensure that customer needs are being translated into prioritized, initiative-level, strategic backlogs, and given to the right teams with the right resources at the right times. Only then can you create flow.

Distribute Decision-Making

Every system of work is contingent on decisions. Some are almost insignificant, a part of the approximately 35,000 we make every day. Do I choose stripes for today's Zoom catchup or plaid? Will my executive stakeholders notice I'm wearing Bermuda shorts if I accidentally stand up on camera? While some will affect the work we do, and the outcomes we achieve, day by day translating into large cumulative impact over time. Others affect those around us in more significant ways: decisions regarding group processes, the way we communicate, and the direction or prioritization of projects.

One person (or one team) can only make so many large-scale decisions per day. Information needs to be gathered, processed, organized, and considered. Opinions need to be debated. When we funnel decisions into the hands of only a few, or create systems where decisions have to be filtered up through layers of hierarchy and then back down to the teams actually doing the work, we create terrible bottlenecks. The process grinds to a halt.

And we can't afford that. Not in a VUCA world.

Agile systems require agile decision-making. That means fast, flexible, and, most importantly, *distributed* decision-making. And to do so, we must build systems of governance that not only enable that distribution but give people the knowledge and tools they need to make the right decisions at the right times. Build trust in people, and design the systems simply to verify the work.

This is the only way to enable a constant and high-speed flow of work. It gives us the capacity for expedient directional decisions, timely interventions, and pivot-point decisions, without the need to double and triple-check with layers upon layers of hierarchy.

Agile and lean ways of working aim for a "close in person, place, and time" method of decision-making. This allows for the necessary decisions to be made conclusively by the people closest to the work, closest to the time that the decision is required, and closest to the mess created by our complex, adaptive systems. Agile Governance asks us to examine how this affects methods of leadership. When decisions are in the hands of smaller teams and individuals, how do leaders enable this? How can they encourage bold decisions? How do they build the guide rails which ensure smart decisions are being made, and that people can learn from and build upon their mistakes? And how might they know when to step back versus when to lean in?

Failure tolerance is important, too. Leaders make mistakes. If you're not building tolerance for failure into the model, then the system will snap back at the first sign of failure. We can conceptually move accountability down the organizational chart, but not in practice, as when something goes wrong our society and culture call for a senior person to be held accountable. For optics.

The bigger the organization, and the bigger the stakeholder set, the harder this gets.

It's not enough to hand the reins of decision-making to teams of hundreds, if not thousands, of workers and expect everything to sort itself out. The accompanying governance must support these new paradigms.

Clarity of Purpose and Intent

What is the purpose of your teams? Not just to create products or work through backlogs, but their ultimate purpose. Do they know what they're working towards, or what their efforts will achieve? Do they understand the intent of their leaders, and of their leaders' leaders? Do you know what it is that *you* must do? In the *Art of Action*[58] Stephen Bungay explores how the most pressing problem in most large-scale organizations today is clarity of outcomes and the ability to align people to that end while ensuring the right level of autonomy across hierarchies. Aligned Autonomy—a property of agile teams adopted by Spotify to great success—helps to enable this clarity of mission.

Given the increasingly VUCA business environment and the collapse of annual planning cycles and fixed three-year strategies,

[58] Bungay, S. (2011). *The Art of Action*. Hachette UK.

agile organizations have increasingly embraced dynamic strategic planning in response to change. Life, and strategic planning, is a constant game of making decisions based on incomplete information. The goal of strategic thinking, or the thought process for deciding which markets to compete in and how, is about trying to assimilate boundless information and make decisions that ensure the company's survival.

However, governance practices aren't necessarily keeping pace. Purpose and intent are changing but the flow of information isn't fast enough. As a result, organizations can't adapt and transform their structure in ways that help to execute strategic change, and so aren't keeping abreast of the organization's outcomes.

Instead, we need to ensure strategy is being decomposed down to the team level. After all, structure follows strategy. We know it in our hearts, but are we internalizing it? Are we building governance to enable it? Are we working to understand how our teams are organized, how their work flows and delivers, and how that aligns with larger strategic needs?

In short, if you want your teams ready and willing to adjust patterns of work to suit the larger organizational intent, you have to do more than ensure that intent is transparent. You have to broadcast it loud and clear.

The Team Codifies its Way of Working

As teams become increasingly agile and adapt their ways of working to suit complex, changing environments, they build stores of specialized knowledge that can't be easily transferred. Their methods of communication, prioritization, and collections of bespoke tools and processes might be exceptionally effective, but passing that wisdom on to others? That's a trickier task.

To correct this, persistent teams should make regular efforts to codify the ways in which they work. Their processes should be described, explored, and shared. Their best ideas should be made transparent and held up to scrutiny.

There are, of course, different types of work and different domains of problems. We don't advocate a one-size-fits-all Way of Working. It never works. Instead, we advocate having core pillars that cross the organization and align the work, while allowing localized creation as to how that work is created (a return to the Aligned Autonomy paradigm).

This achieves a number of things. It helps spread knowledge across organizations and allows teams to clearly compare and contrast their ways of working. This builds safe spaces for the distribution and development of new ideas, and an atmosphere of continuous improvement. In fact, there's a well-known axiom in the Toyota Production System related to this and attributed to founder Taiichi Ohno: "Without standard work there can be no kaizen (improvement)."

It also allows stakeholders, suppliers, and customers an insight into how the sausage is made. In Software Development, and much of the 21st century knowledge-based industry, this is critical but because it is often hidden work, there's no way to *see* the factory floor. Opening up that floor means more accurately providing those teams with the resources and other support to ensure the organization meets its goals. Just as importantly, it allows the team's methods, their IP and frameworks, to persist after people move on from the team.

With these four imperatives firmly in place, is it wise to simply stand back and let the teams build their own patterns of work, communications, codification, and so on? Not necessarily. Even in a highly agile, highly autonomous environment, guide rails are a must. Think of them less as constraints and more as codified signposts that help autonomous teams know they're heading in the right direction. This also functions as an assurance mechanism.

Models like the Remote Agility Framework, which we discuss in greater detail in Chapters 12.1-12.5, can help accomplish this. They support teams in understanding the larger goals, strategy and direction, and *how* to get the work done. This frees them up to figure out the *what*: the actual ways they'll be getting the work done on the ground. Using patterns like the Remote Agility Framework also gives confidence to leaders (and the larger organizational mindset) that they can stand back and trust the teams, the people closest to the work and the customer, to know best how they work and how the work gets done the best.

In the same manner, teams will understand better than anyone which information they need to thrive, and which information is superfluous. We've discussed transparency and radical openness in communication before, but that doesn't mean that every team needs to know everything all the time. In fact, absolute transparency (from a cost and time perspective) is almost impossible.

This means that trusting teams to do the work also means trusting them to seek out the information they need from inside a transparent system, instead of forcing it upon them.

As per Team Topologies: *"Many organizations assume that more communication is always better, but this is not really the case. What we need is focused communications between specific teams."* [59]

Dynamic Re-teaming When Your Environment Changes

Once you have the methods, they are not static. That's also the essence of agility: responding to change is, after all, one of the core values of agile and that applies to your ways of working. Many organizations are learning this and seeing the value in building

---

[59] Skelton, M. and Pais, M. (2019). *Team topologies: organizing business and technology teams for fast flow*. Portland, Oregon: It Revolution.

organizational competency for re-design and re-launching of teams when the strategy changes, opportunities arise, or the thing you are working towards solving moves from novel to known and the work changes in nature, maybe becoming repeatable, and can be executed differently.

This can mean becoming a candidate for increased automation and even the use of machine learning to take on more and more of the human activity, which means needing to change how you work and how you govern that new system of work. It happens at different levels, from the small, localized team right up to the business unit. In our view, you always need to consider whether you are organized in the right way to solve your problems most efficiently and effectively, and whether your operating model is right for the same reasons. This holds true for how you govern your systems of work. As you apply change to your operating and teaming models, it will apply pressure to how you govern the system, requiring you to adapt in response.

What we see more often than not, though, is that it doesn't happen. The work gets harder to execute, layers of process and process governance are added where they're not needed, and the system slows down. Being able to change your operating and teaming model is a core capability that is often missed and ends up the province of consulting firms. In a VUCA world, our view is that you need strong internal transformation capability so that you can be constantly inspecting and adapting your own ways of working to avoid the big bang transformations of the past. If you're not moving forward then you're going backwards, because your competition does not stand still.

Knowing your Methods Matters

When you boil all these concepts down, you're left with a series of questions to ask of yourself and your governance methodologies.

106

Consider: are you using the ways your teams are organized to guide your strategy, or vice-versa? How does your governance allow for teams to seek and obtain the information they need? Do they have clarity of purpose and a clear flow of work so they can accurately determine what it is they need to know and when? Have you built systems that allow teams the authority to make relevant, timely decisions and move forward on projects without losing time and energy to approval processes?

Or is everyone struggling through a sea of residual control mechanisms that are slowly and silently devaluing and reverting your agile transformations?

9

Stanchion #4: Data-Driven Reasoning

Most humans are right 30% of the time—maybe 40% if we're generous. Or, if you're a fan of Anchorman and Brian Fontana[60], "They've done studies, you know. Sixty percent of the time, it works every time." **With** this high degree of inaccuracy, relying on our mental models, experience, and intuition is risky. In human behavioral research, it has been found that human decision-making is strongly biased by unconscious mental processes, often referred to as "System 1"[61], which is fast, instinctive, and emotional. It sometimes produces good outcomes quickly, and sometimes causes us to make irrational choices. Our rational mind is referred to as "System 2", and it is slower, more deliberate, and more logical, but it rarely intervenes. Fear of loss influences human decisions more than expectation of gains. This bias affects people's choices and decisions in risky situations, like whether to buy insurance, accept lawsuit settlements, gamble, or invest in projects and initiatives.

Creating accessible, transparent, real-time data to generate insights and make decisions can increase your decision success rate. You can't improve if you don't have a benchmark to improve against. You can't tell which teams are working well and which teams are struggling based on vibes or intuition. Don't get us wrong. Opinions are great, and even though early forms of

---

[60] Dreamworks Pictures, Anchorman: The Legend of Ron Burgundy, 2004, Brian Fontana https://www.youtube.com/watch?v=pjvQFtlNQ-M
[61] Thinking, Fast and Slow: Kahneman, Daniel: Amazon.com.au: Books. (n.d.).

Artificial Intelligence are already becoming part of our workflow and decision-making, insights are still generated by people.

However, everyone has their own opinions, shaped by their own mental models. Upping the challenge, comparing and contrasting data collected from teams with different ways of working, is no simple task, and maintaining visibility over teams (both as a measure of performance but also to ensure teams are getting what they need when they need it) is a key function of good governance.

Most work that we are focused on when we consider Agile Governance is knowledge work, and knowledge work is generally hidden work. Global Transformation Lead, Mirco Hering, has a saying he likes to use whenever the topic of knowledge work comes up: "It's not a factory anymore!"[62] We can't walk down to the shop floor, peer across the supply lines and conveyor belts, gather inputs and watch a project move closer to "Done". We can still go to the gemba, but what we want to see is the progress of the creation of value. We talked about this in *Chapter 7, Sensible Transparency*—an output of Transparency is data.

Some choose to measure projects against that classic workhorse, the Iron Triangle, which balances time, cost, and scope (or sometimes swaps scope for quality). Some organizations have added other key elements and created the concept of success sliders: adding quality and stakeholders amongst other key measures of progress. Others prefer more personal measures: customer satisfaction or team engagement. But are these measures actually helping us to gather the necessary and timely information needed to make directionally guiding decisions? Are they helping us take the next best action in a fast-paced world, where we don't have the luxury of waiting for project post implementation reviews (PIRs)

---

[62] Mirco Hering Blog Site; Not a Factory Anymore: *https://notafactoryanymore.com*

that can help shape the next right decisions?

It's more common to see these sorts of measures in place when we have a governance model that relies on intermittent (monthly, quarterly, or even longer) status reporting, where large gaps between reports allow for a gentle massaging of data to produce whatever narrative is needed at the time. A need for more resources can be countered with reports of cost blowouts. If teams need more time, management can point to schedules being pushed. And so on, and so on. We can generally find a statistic or data point to support most decisions. What we often see in this sort of situation is "watermelon reporting", where everything is purportedly green until you carve it open and find the core is nothing but red.

On that note, there's a good argument to be made that every project should start red and stay red until it's completed its first real increment and is delivered to users[63]. Every new project or program is an assumption. It's an informed, educated bet, but it's still a bet. Full of risk assumptions and untested ideas. So how can we, after time spent drawing diagrams and crafting PowerPoint slides, think it's green when nothing has been delivered yet? Referring back to our old friend, General Von Moltke, even he knew in 1809 that, "No plan of operations reaches with any certainty beyond the first encounter with the enemy's main force." As soon as you start the work, the work changes.

As teams become increasingly agile, our measures must become more agile to match. Instead of measuring total cost, time, or scope, we can look to predictability, delivery, and improvement. We can map out our system of work and the states it goes through to get to Done. It's useful to systemize this process by adopting tools that allow us to trace our work and manage cross team

---

[63] Gadzinski, Phil. *Projects and the fear of RED*. [online] Available at: https://www.linkedin.com/pulse/projects-fear-red-phillip-gadzinski/ [Accessed 28 Jul. 2023].

collaboration and dependencies. This means we can measure lead time, cycle time, flow, flow efficiency, and many other important guiding measures. Combined, these measures help us to understand our performance and how we might intervene to uplift that performance. We're personally fans of the DORA metrics from the DevOps Research and Assessment Team[64]. However, you need to find the metrics that best work for the governance model you're trying to build.

To paraphrase Watts S. Humphrey, if every company is a technology company, then the best predictors of organizational success are the ability to meet and exceed the following measures:

- Deployment Frequency: How often an organization successfully releases to production;
- Lead Time for Changes: The amount of time it takes a "commit" to get into production;
- Change Failure Rate: The percentage of deployments causing a failure in production;
- Time to Restore Service: How long it takes an organization to recover from a failure in production.

If you're looking for a starting point to understand how to gather this data and apply it properly, we recommend *The Phoenix Project* (Kim, Spafford & Behr, 2013) or *Accelerate* (Kim, Humble & Forsgren, 2018).

In fact, there are layers upon layers of metrics we may want to use. They can be related to Enterprise Strategy: things that are baked into the Annual Operating Plans and objectives and are often

[64] Google Cloud Blog. (n.d.). *Using the Four Keys to measure your DevOps performance.* [online] Available at: https://cloud.google.com/blog/products/devops-sre/using-the-four-keys-to-measure-your-devops-performance.

tied to Management Bonuses (meaning they get the most attention). They can exist on the System Change level, and inform us as to how we're progressing towards the investment in the delivery of change initiatives; i.e., programs, projects, and things that drive the outcomes in the Enterprise strategy. They can be like the DORA metrics above, which (despite the fact that they can be aggregated into an organizational view) come from the teams and their performance. In fact, these metrics (if created and managed centrally) enable us to drill into team-level performance as well, thus giving us the data we need for making those directionally guided next-best decisions.

These sorts of measures also help us compare agile vs non-agile teams, tracking their performance side by side when they're working together on common outcomes. Note: when we say "non-agile", we understand that, in a modern organization, all teams must at least exhibit the principles of agility. It's not a binary decision, even though you often see the choice appear as agile or waterfall delivery. The ways of working can differ between teams to such a degree that some appear or operate in a manner that's markedly more agile than others. This creates difficulty when it comes to aligning their growth and progression against broader organizational outcomes. Every project needs an element of agility, even if you have long-lived sequential base plans, whether the solution space is known and repeatable, to interact with other work going on in the broader ecosystem. No team is an island.

This need to clearly trace work with data and make that next directionally guiding decision across multiple ways of working is especially critical when we no longer have neatly defined stage gates or end dates to drive reporting. We need dynamic measures, adaptive measures, intelligent measures. We need data that's as clever as our teams.

We also need data that's already in a form, or as close to it as possible, that helps us form insights and make rapid decisions. To put it simply, if the data you're collecting takes so long to interpret that the opportunity to make a powerful decision is lost, then the data degrades in its efficacy. The best decisions are always timely. Hence the push to move away from 100-page status reports and instead take people to the gemba—the actual place of work.

In a physical space, going to the gemba would imply a walk through the manufacturing floor, or a boots-on-the-ground consultation with engineers in their place of work. In remote work or knowledge work, this might instead mean going directly to the workflow management system or information radiator/kanban board and directly engaging with the team doing the work against the way they visualize and trace their work—their Information Radiator, to borrow from Dr. Alistair Cockburn. Whatever it takes to get the data directly from the source! This not only increases the pace of decision-making but also decreases the lead time for gathering the right data. Not to mention the wasted time we so often see thanks to the demand for data presented in crisp, perfect PowerPoint decks. No offense to our design teams, but there's immense value in ditching the polished status reports in favor of raw progress information.

However, what do we do once we have this data? How do we use it to drive our decision-making? There are four key elements that can help you carve this flood of data into useful, applicable information that aids in making fast, critical decisions.

Digital Tools are Essential

Even before COVID-19 forced most modern workplaces into a new remote-work paradigm, the technology sector had been in a state of transition towards digital workflow management systems being the norm. They're the critical enablers of shared knowledge in the 21st century workplace, which is crucial for teams of teams developing complex and complicated systems. Being Australian, one of our homegrown technology success stories was built on the back of this transition and led the global evolution. We speak, of course, of Atlassian[65], Jira[66], and the supporting applications that have evolved around it. It's all been in the service of uplifting the way we deliver work—they are essentially selling pickaxes to miners, often a better path to success than doing the mining yourself.

We're sure you're already aware that any time you have two or more people working on a single outcome, they need ways to collaborate and share their work and progress. The larger the team or the wider the spread, the more critical that workflow stack becomes. Reliability, planning, predictability, alignment, traceability of progress… all of this collapses without our modern suites of digital tools, which help us visualize the unseen and support our new, digital, remote work models.

If you're not already trading in your real-world, physical tools for digital, you're a long way behind the curve. There will always be a place for the physical—especially when you have people coming together in the same place to work and collaborate—but the sustained move to remote and hybrid working demands that we think digital first. Emerging data[67] shows that the creative and knowledge-type workforce is settling into an approximately 2:3 split between remote and in-person work. In other words, up to 40% of your team might not be working physically together at any time.

---

[65] An Australian software company that develops products for software developers, project managers and other software development teams. For more information see https://www.atlassian.com

[66] A proprietary bug tracking and agile project management developed by Atlassian.

[67] Barrero, J., Bloom, N. and Davis, S. (2023). *The Evolution of Working from Home.* [online] Available at: https://wfhresearch.com/wp-content/uploads/2023/07/SIEPR1.pdf.

Therefore, everything must be digitized first.

Data Trumps Opinion

Now that we have the data and the digital tools to share it, what do we do with it?

We need to make it visible. We need to make it clear. And we need to use it in ways that replaces (or at the very least, augments) opinion-based decision-making.

In other words, we need to dump monthly PowerPoints showing our group progress against the outcome, or the extent of the backlog. Everyone has access to that data already. We can see the work in progress, what's been delivered, our lead times, our flow, our predictability metrics. So, let's have useful discussions about what to do with that data and how it might affect the decisions we make day-to-day, moment-to-moment.

As humans, we rely on pre-existing mental models to make decisions. When we need to quickly assess a problem and make a call, we draw upon a variety of elements: our past history and learning, who we trust, our perception of the domain of the problem, the sound bite we heard or overheard at the water cooler, the comment from a peer at the coffee shop that we just can't shake, our own heuristics and patterns, our learned behaviors, and so on. Even our own status and ego come into play when determining how we view, shape, and decide how to use the gathered information. No two people view a problem in the same way—everything is shaped by our individual perspectives and histories.

What data from the source does is break through the lens of our personal bias and provide a common starting point from which to make the next decision. It might not guarantee two or more people come to the same conclusion or make the same decision, but it does mean that everyone is standing at the same starting line.

Improve Constantly and Forever... Visibly

We're fans of W. Edwards Deming and his fourteen points model of Total Quality Management[68]. As much as things change, some tend to stay the same, and we've found that many of Deming's quotes, and much of his work, to be timeless. Of the fourteen points, which aim to improve a company's quality and productivity, it's number five that's most relevant to this section: "Improve constantly and forever the system of production and service, to improve quality and productivity, and thus constantly decrease costs."

However, you can't do any of this without data. Deming knew this as well: "In God we trust, all others bring data."

No complaints here! The systems of work that many modern organizations have adopted, plus the accompanying digital tool sets, provide us with an incredible amount of data on the performance of teams and the delivery of creative work. Work that, in the past, remained buried within the monthly PowerPoint deck and the Work Breakdown Sheet (WBS). Hard data means we can have conversations and make decisions from a position of truth, which in turn allows us to build trust—in our leaders making the right decisions, in our team members doing the right work at the right time, and in our customers having the necessary information to give us accurate feedback on the products we're building for them.

Note that we've already discussed how total transparency can be a double-edged sword. However, we'll say it again: everyone knowing everything all of the time can be overwhelming and may even stifle innovation. Plus, we've found that the acquisition costs of this knowledge and information likely far exceed the benefits for decision-making. If we want people to constantly improve and

---

[68] Dr Edwards Deming: The New Economics - 14 Points for Management; Out of The Crisis (MIT Press) (pp. 23-24)https://deming.org/explore/fourteen-points

develop more accurate forecasts, we need to make sure they have transparency into everything they need *without* drowning them in irrelevant data. The cost of extracting and visualizing data in both time and money terms must not exceed the value that it creates for the decision maker. Part of putting it into practice is you must budget for design, implementation, and maintenance of digital decision support environments.

Directional Decisions Informed by Instrumentation

As discussed above, we now have the tools, which collect relevant data, to support a constant improvement model. So, what now?

We use that data to guide decisions, of course.

Speed of execution is one of the critical factors in effective agility, and speed is governed almost entirely by the flow of information. Without the right data at the right time and in the right format to make those directionally guiding decisions, leaders find it challenging to let go of micro decision-making and control. This is compounded in organizations lacking a strong delegation culture. In an environment such as this, we see long lead times for decisions, thus increasing delays across the system of work. This directly impacts our level of agility, as well as our responsiveness to change, or when new information is surfaced.

We previously referred to the Westrum model of Organizational Culture, defined by Ron Westrum[69]. Westrum's theory proposes that organizations with better information flow tend to operate more effectively and exhibit higher quality decision-making. His model, also known as the Generative model, focuses on the goal and the outcome, i.e., the core purpose of the organization. Data informed by the instrumentation we have available in the modern workforce gives us the ability to implement

---

[69] Westrum, R (1988) *A Typology of Organizational Cultures*

117

this model, or models like it.

The more open, accessible, real-time, and accurate our data, the better our decisions. Just as we keep one eye on our instrumentation when driving a car—using our speedometer and fuel gauge to track progress, and our temperature gauge and engine lights to keep aware of potential faults—so should we keep one eye on our team and department data when working on projects.

The problem we sometimes encounter is that, even when teams have access to all the data they need, they often don't use it for planning. Intuition and personal experience can trump the facts, and this leads to teams getting it wrong. Deming was right and still is—data trumps opinion. As humans, we tend to trust our instincts ahead of the data and make decisions based on what we perceive to be true. However, as we know, everyone's truth is different. There's a view used in Organizational and Relationship Systems Coaching[70] (ORSC™) that "everyone is right… but only partially". What data does is align on facts and bring people's different truths closer together. It also breaks some of the mythology we uncover when decisions are based on our own mental models instead of on data. It can be challenging as a human to look at the hard data and find that your opinion was wrong, and it takes a high degree of self-awareness to accept a conflicting idea, investigate it, and maybe change one's opinion. Data is the key enabler to help us make better, more directionally aligned calls.

What the data also allows us to do is increase the likelihood that our decisions are going to be more accurate. We reduce the decision-making batch size by making those calls more frequently, by gaining faster feedback, and thus lower our risk profiles. This helps us make smaller, directionally aligned decisions more often.

This, of course, doesn't apply to every problem domain. In a

---

[70] *For more information, see CRR Global: https://crrglobal.com/about/orsc/*

complex adaptive system, which is where we work, data is often either unavailable or just not useful. The Cynefin domain thinking implies that we don't even know the problem yet, so we can hardly start applying historical information to make informed decisions. Instead, we need lots of sensors and probes to generate information quickly. These allow us to make the next best decision. Modern instrumentation allows us to do this better—if we apply it effectively.

The philosophy of Deming is over forty years old, but we believe it still holds true today. Technology has changed, economics has changed, but these fundamental ways of thinking are rock-solid. What's frustrating is that, as a collective industry, we've had four decades to internalize this knowledge, however, we are only now really recognizing and adapting our ways of thinking and working. As Steve Denning says, we're now in the age of agile and agile is a management revolution[71].

No data, no agility.

We're rapidly approaching a point where that adaptation will no longer be optional (if we haven't passed that point already). The last decade has seen an explosion in the variety, availability, and use of digital tools, giving us access to data, information, and insights we never had before. This means that the ability to get system instrumentation from your teams and use it for decision-making is no longer a nice bonus. It's baseline, entry-level thinking. Agile 101. A core foundation that allows you to build real agility at scale. Only once you have that baseline can you build the fast-paced data delivery required for persistent, dynamic teams.

Above all, remember this fundamental principle: "To make

[71] *Denning, S. (2018). The age of agile - how smart companies are transforming the way work gets done. New York, Ny Amacom American Management Association.*

119

Data-Driven Reasoning, you need the right data. To have the right data that is useful, you need to measure the right things."

10

Stanchion #5: Humanity
as the Cornerstone

Traditional governance seeks predictability, stability, security. It's static, slow to respond to change, and generally unwieldy. As such, it can't be effective unless the existing systems stay static as well. Traditional governance is also often a very linear process, with long delays between opportunities for sharing information and feedback. This time delay, in turn, leads to the need to generate excessive amounts of information. We're all familiar with the mantra, "Less is more." Well, in traditional governance, more is more. None of this is suitable for the modern VUCA world, in which long-term success thrives on fast feedback.

Compliance and regulation demand strict adherence to statutory processes and mandates. Many of the industries we work with are heavily regulated by government entities, with specific goals of preserving the norms of society. Take for example the Australian Prudential Regulation Authority. "The Australian Prudential Regulation Authority (APRA) is an independent statutory authority that supervises institutions across banking, insurance and superannuation and promotes financial system stability in Australia."[72]

---

[72] Sourced from https://www.apra.gov.au/

If you want to understand the constraints placed on organizations by regulators, which give rise to governance approaches and standards, start by examining what the Industry Regulator seeks to achieve. For example, "APRA's role is to protect the Australian community by establishing and enforcing legally binding standards that apply to these APRA-regulated entities. In supervising these institutions, APRA seeks to ensure these entities carefully (or prudently) manage their businesses in order to protect the interests, in particular, of bank depositors, insurance policyholders, and superannuation members. APRA's primary mandate is to ensure that APRA-regulated entities have sufficient financial means to meet their obligations to customers: that deposits are safe; that insurers have sufficient funds to pay claims; and that superannuation trustees are managing people's money well. APRA does this by focusing, as much as possible, on preventing harm before it occurs, and by taking pre-emptive action when problems are identified."

This means that the Regulator has a key role to play in system-wide governance. Their goal is system stability and consumer protection, but at the least possible cost, and not in all circumstances. They aim to avoid overly prescriptive regulation that prevents business from taking place. Ironically, there are specific examples where regulation is actually removing humanity, such as in aged care provision. One bad apple creates administration for a whole industry, the job ceases to be about caring for people, and instead it becomes about ticking boxes.

What does this mean when you throw one hundred, one thousand or even one hundred thousand people into the mix, all with differing opinions, motivations, histories, ethical foundations, and methodologies? You can begin to understand why many systems of governance seem to want to minimize or strip away the humanity of their teams. There are Prudential Standards, Prudential

Guidelines and Reporting Standards… and not much that is human centric. In fact, many systems of Governance eschew the carrot and instead use a stick based on these regulatory/compliance standards to expedite or block work, which in turn creates unnecessary tension.

In our experience, if you approach these regulatory bodies with a plan to meet their requirements through a more human lens, you may find that they're more fluid than you expected. This is a humanistic approach of "intent versus permission", rather than the traditional governing methods of "just get it done and ignore the impacts to the organization and its people".

Agile Governance, on the other hand, sees humanity as the cornerstone of good business. It values humanistic methods of governance over the more mechanistic, rule-based and non-adaptive methods, which aligns with the Agile Manifesto valuing individuals and interactions over processes and tools. It values individuality, and seeks to encourage and enhance the unique characteristics, skills, and viewpoints that each person brings to the table. Concepts like trust, responsibility, democracy, fairness, and humility are core to human systems. There are specific examples where the regulator of an industry will meet with the regulated to work through the intent and application of the regulation, and then verify adoption. This happens often in banking and insurance, for instance. We would view this as a more human approach: seeking to collaborate effectively given that our goals should be aligned.

We would argue that this isn't an alternative to traditional governance so much as it is the *only* way to create effective governance. You can't legislate the humanity out of humans. Apply all the mechanistic controls you like: processes, standardization, phase-gating, micro-task allocation, management, and so on. Humans will always be the blip in the radar, the ghost in the machine. The more you attempt to stifle or strip out the human element, the worse your governance becomes: more rigid, stratified, and more likely to crumble once it clashes against any complexity. These forms of governance aren't emergent, adaptive, nor responsive—it's the *people* who bring that ability to respond, adapt, and embrace variation.

Transitioning to a human-centric system of governance doesn't change the fundamental goals of that system: the intent and the outcome. The *why* of setting practices and methods to control and report on work is also unchanged. We want to change the how and the what, and even then, we're not asking for a complete reinvention. Just a shift, a little jump to the left. Some of the how will still be constrained by the same requirements and regulations, and the what will be guided by enabling constraints. Some of these constraints may be preventative. Others may give structure and guidance to your new Governance model. Yet, inside these constraints, we allow people to explore what is needed to meet these requirements while minimizing what is not. This is, in the words of Pat Reed[73] (and commonly used in Lean parlance), a quest for Minimal Viable Everything.

This is why we're so intent on finding the people who actually do the work and enabling them to become the true governance custodians of the system. They're the ones who know what the customer wants, how to give them what they need, what the needs of the system are, and how to best enable one another to deliver. We don't set them adrift without a compass. Instead, we set out clear conditions and constraints and allow people the space to meet them in varying ways. So long as the outcome is achieved within these boundaries, everyone is happy. This flexibility, this agility, is critical because the nature of modern work varies so much and so

---

[73] Pat Reed is a brilliant Business Agility Consultant with a storied career that's taken her from forensic analysis, to working for Disney, and now to agile coaching organization SoftEd. Connect with her at https://www.linkedin.com/in/reedpat

quickly. Trying to place prohibitive governance on an exploratory problem domain invites failure. Trying to have light governance and controls in highly regulated industries that require near-zero fault tolerance will also invite failure.

When we discuss what placing humanity at the cornerstone of good governance entails, a common reaction is: what about oversight? Can't you see the risks in simply handing over the keys to the entire system?

That's not what we're advocating for at all. Oversight is a necessity in any system. However, it should be lightweight and supportive, as opposed to unwieldy and restrictive to the point of choking the system and becoming an obstacle to work. It also needs inherent variability in the problem domain it's trying to secure. We want to change the understanding of oversight to one based first and foremost in trust. That means trusting in the training, coaching, guide rails, and data-collection systems as well. It means changing the controls so that when teams are audited (or audit themselves), they're measuring against things that matter.

All of this combines into a governance system where teams have faith in the information at hand, can confidently make directional decisions and provide their intent to leadership, and where established systems collect and report data continuously.

When a system like this is in place and working well, leaders can apply the "trust but verify" approach, popularized during the Reagan era of political management. There is an inherent need for leaders to do their due diligence and confirm the facts. But this doesn't imply a lack of trust in their workers. In fact, it creates an understanding that trust is a bi-directional flow of information.

Trust in People

None of this can happen unless we ensure that the people doing the work have the right levels of guide rails, clarity, competence, and capabilities. Where everyone has inherent trust that the people beside them, above them, and below them are doing the right thing.

This approach is complementary to "Leading with Intent", discussed in Chapter 6, *Conductive Leadership*. In fact, this stanchion has a symbiotic relationship with the other stanchions in that all of them must be in place for it to be effective, and they in turn require it for their own success.

11

The Virtual Obeya

When we were first developing our theories and practice of Agile Governance, the fundamental query we kept coming back to was: How can we ensure that information is kept clear and accessible, thus enabling the expeditious and adaptable decision-making required in today's VUCA world?

From our experiences over the years, we've come to enjoy and appreciate the advantages of creating a physical space dedicated to the transmission and sharing of information. A space like this— known as an Obeya, the origins of which we'll explore shortly—is crucial to creating Agile Governance in any organization. But today's business context requires a digital solution to the same question.

The problem we kept running into while answering that first question was that we were juggling two issues at the same time: how to keep information clear and accessible, and how to facilitate the best parts of an Obeya in a digital space. Serendipitously, just as we were debating these problems, we were afforded the unique opportunity to become co-creators of the "Remote Agility Framework (Remote:af)"[74].

In fact, it was the (virtually overnight) move to remote working for millions of people that allowed us to dedicate serious time to

---

[74]The Remote AF Co: building a method for organizations to evolve;
https://www.remoteaf.co

the development of Remote:af. This framework emerged from paying very close attention to COVID-19 and the signals that showed, if one was paying attention, how the evolution of the virus mimicked the patterns of the 1918 Spanish Flu. The epidemiology and clinical features, as well as the resulting social and cultural issues, reveal great similarities. Their outbreak pattern led the team we were working with, and others, to hypothesize a similar duration and death burden for COVID-19, in the absence of effective vaccines or innovative treatments. This meant that some of the ways the world changed in the wake of COVID-19 were predictable. It was Andrew Blain, co-founder of Remote:af, who was one of the first to anticipate these changes, and take the initiative to move agile and his frameworks into a purely digital context.

This opportunity gave us the chance to incorporate the Five Stanchions as well as our thoughts on the fledgling Virtual Obeya into the framework (we'll chat more on this in the following chapters). The next few chapters, in which we explore the Virtual Obeya, are deeply rooted in the work we did while creating the Remote Agility Framework, and we want to acknowledge Remote:af for kindly allowing us to publish those ideas.

Let's begin with a brief overview of the Obeya—its past, present, and future. Obeya, meaning "large room" in Japanese, is a single space where leaders can come together to collaborate on solving complex problems.

Although the term has roots in modern Japanese culture, the concept has been practiced in many cultures for over two and a half millennia. The Chinese, Greeks, and Egyptians, among others, all recognized the value in creating an arena for debates, a forum for productive discussions, or a super-charged environment where distractions are minimized and ideas fly so thick and fast that solutions can be plucked out of the air. A war room, a command center, or the bridge of the USS Enterprise.

We now use Obeya in a management context. The Obeya room might contain team leads, department heads, engineers, managers, etc. Stepping into an Obeya room, you know it's time to focus. You'll be working with leaders from technology, legal, sales, human resources, and more. The agenda is clear: a single problem to solve that needs input and expertise from every area of the business. It could be a product that needs designing, an initiative that needs to be launched, or a strategy that's gotten lost in the weeds. It could be the creation of a mission team designed purposefully to achieve a valuable outcome.

Crucial information is clearly displayed. The end goal is established. The mood is high. Everyone is united and aligned; nobody is there to score points. Everyone is elbow-to-elbow, sharing their perspectives. Hierarchy is flattened. The team acts as one. In the Stanchion of Data-Driven Reasoning, we declare that the more open, accessible, real-time, and accurate our data, the better the decisions. And, just as we keep one eye on our instrumentation when driving a car—using our speedometer and fuel gauge to track progress, and our temperature gauge and engine lights to keep aware of potential faults—so should we keep one eye on our team and department data when working on projects. That makes the Obeya an organization's Heads-Up Display.

This isn't a radical concept for most modern organizations. In fact, even if they never use the term Obeya, they have the capacity to create something that functions similarly. You'll often see this in emergency situations: a crisis center is spun up almost instantly. People are directed to work collaboratively, often across functions and boundaries, to quickly work through the scenario and solve the issue. We got to see this in action a few years back while working with a large Australian Telecommunications organization to define the drivers and impediments to designing an enterprise agile transformation. The common call out was that the organization was able to respond quickly and work well in a crisis, so how might they capture that intent and collaboration more often? And sustain it? One key element contributing to the success of this approach was their use of a "war room", functionally an Obeya. The problem was that, although this was a place full of information and access to communication, and even though it was open to people spread across not just Australia but the entire globe, it wasn't optimized for digitality.

An Obeya that's optimized for its users and context can be a magical place. High communication, high collaboration, and everyone working in alignment towards a common goal. If you haven't enjoyed the unique atmosphere of an Obeya room before, this might all sound a little fanciful. That many leaders in one space with no arguments or miscommunications? All the relevant information on display without people becoming overloaded? Isn't that just another massive meeting? We'll admit, making an Obeya function well isn't simply a matter of throwing a handful of leaders into a room. There are definitely best practices and principles at play that make the Obeya work, and we'll be exploring them shortly. But all we want to do for the moment is give you that visual: a big space, filled with experts and information, all aligned and rowing in the same direction.

However, with remote/hybrid ways of working become the norm, and most Australian and global organizations landing on at least a 3:2 office/home split in the knowledge worker domains, getting all the necessary people into a single Obeya type space is becoming more and more difficult. At the same time, it's increasingly necessary for organizations (and people at all levels of those organizations) to have a place where they can absorb the information—data, opinions, trade secrets, unique perspectives, and so on—that they need to do their jobs. And let's not forget, that information is endless! How often do you see or hear the quote: "I'm drowning in a sea of data yet starving for knowledge"? History tends to repeat in different spheres of human endeavor. As Coleridge wrote: "Water, water, everywhere, And all the boards did shrink; Water, water, everywhere, Nor any drop to drink!"[75]

The ability to synthesize, cut through the noise, and create meaningful insights that are actionable, can't happen without the collaboration of *people*. Which means, as we covered in *Chapter 9 Data-Driven Reasoning*, availability and transparency. It also means, as we covered in *Chapter 10 Humanity as the Cornerstone*, that people are the necessary ingredient to drive that collaboration.

So, we need to make the Obeya virtual.

At this point, we guarantee there's at least one reader asking: "Isn't that just a more organized Zoom meeting?"

If only it were that simple.

Let's dive deeper into what makes an Obeya unique. It's not just a place to mingle. It's not only a space where information can be shared. It's more than a communal hub for focused discussion. And it has to be more than the centers of communication that are thrown up quickly in times of crisis. That model must be made ubiquitous, stable, and fundamental to the organization's culture. Its information must transcend time and place in this distributed world. Finally, it must serve as an effective replacement to the current governance approach of 100-page status reports that are out of date by the time they're submitted.

An Obeya is a place that *radiates* information: from people to people, from the organization to the organization, and from country to country. It supports multiple perspectives simultaneously while facilitating cross-communication. It adapts to

---

[75] Samuel Taylor Coleridge (1798). *Rime Of The Ancient Mariner.*

the needs of users instead of asking them to adapt to the limitations of the room. It enables autonomy through directional alignment, rather than dictating alignment by removing autonomy. It's more than just a modified SharePoint site or a confluence wiki page. In fact, it's not an exaggeration to say that it's the missing ingredient that brings agile to life.

When you compare this vision of an Obeya against the core values of agile, you may feel there's a conflict with the statement, "Working Software (Things) over Comprehensive Documentation". We disagree; a Virtual Obeya doesn't conflict with this notion. The Obeya values people and interactions over documentation, but recognizes the need to record the conversations, the agreements, and the decisions made by people and processes, while individuals are interacting with each other. How often have you asked somebody for further information about a recent decision and gotten the reply, "We're agile. We don't do documentation!" It's frustrating and causes a high degree of friction and tension in the overall system. In fact, it creates uncertainty, reduces trust, leads to increased governance and slows down decision-making—the exact opposite outcome of what adopting agile is meant to achieve. We prefer to look at the preposition *over*. People, working software, and good outcomes are more important than documentation. But documentation is still important, and an Obeya can help to capture that.

All of these factors combine to form a space that creates connective tissue throughout an organization. The processing center at the heart of the nervous system, if you will. Just as our nerve endings let us gather information, it's the brain that brings all the synapses and nerve endings together. A single place that uses all of the organization's senses to provide information. Which in turn guides those directionally aligned decisions necessary for a 21st century organization's success.

You can see why, as we noted earlier, the Virtual Obeya is an essential part of Agile Governance.

You can also see why building a Virtual Obeya is more complex than an online chat with bonus breakout rooms. Many of the most ubiquitous online communication platforms (Zoom, Teams, Google Meets, and whatever else has launched by the time this book lands in your hands) aim to recreate a traditional, top-down meeting structure. One person (or a small team) controls, presents, and dictates the pace. Information is not radiated but funneled from the few to the many. Conversations are a series of one-on-one engagements and cross-communication is discouraged or disabled entirely, which makes directional alignment difficult. If you're not part of the channel/chat, or aren't familiar with the structure, information remains hard to come by. Want to get that crucial information for yourself? Then you're relying upon individuals to share it with you, and finding those individuals isn't always easy.

What we find with platforms like Teams and Zoom is that they essentially replicate the physical world—complete with the same hierarchy and limitations—without daring to imagine what a truly digital-centric approach could accomplish.

The Virtual Obeya is separate from the status quo. It allows us to imagine something different.

Something new.

Something necessary.

To figure out how we can create an effective Virtual Obeya, let's start by digging into the makeup of a good Obeya. We can begin with four areas called "Mados" that, combined, create the Obeya as a whole. We use the term Mados (Japanese for window) as they are transparent panes through which we can peer into the organization's information flow.

These Mados are:

- Strategy;
- Work;
- Data; and
- Culture.

We'll discuss them in summary:

The Strategy Mado: a window into how strategy is decomposed across the organization. This helps us understand not just the directional alignment of remote teams, but how those teams are being aligned. To facilitate organizational strategy, we need to create or enable a system that enables information to flow back to strategy planning teams, creates visibility onto the strategic intent so clear and total that everyone from the cleaner to the executive understands the why behind strategy and how it links to delivery, and enables expedient, informed, and strategically aligned directional decisions/interventions.

The Work Mado: how we create visibility in a virtual environment. It allows us to visualize the work portfolio across individual and multiple teams, programs, or areas of the organization. It gathers concrete data from teams, teams of teams, and the enterprise, and weaves it into a single, interconnected system of information that can be used to guide strategic decisions, encourage transparency and alignment, and provide real-time lead and lag indicators of business performance.

The Data Mado: all about aggregating data on the progress, performance, and flow efficiency of the organization. This is why we call it the underpinning Mado—without it, the other Mados would teeter and collapse. It's a window into how the sausage gets made—the metrics behind decisions both major and minor. Getting this data organized and visible is integral to peeling away the layers of organizational information and reporting detritus and sourcing the critical data needed to enable fact-based and data-driven reasoning.

The Culture Mado: is a window into the health of an organization (both the personal, team, and team-of-teams), their social connections, external interactions, and working hours and agreements from the enterprise level all the way down to the individual. When this information is visible and accessible, leaders can proactively use it to understand the behaviors that are expected, accepted, and agreed upon within the organization. They can examine and understand team interactions both internally and externally. Leaders can also learn how teams grow, learn, and maintain excellence.

Let's briefly discuss some commonalities between the Mados (and in turn, Obeyas).

To create any of the four Mados, a higher order of information is required. We covered the intent of these in *Chapter 9 Data-Driven Reasoning*. Breaking down further these include:

- Strategy and its decomposition into objectives for vertical connectivity—the "Why"
- Kanban systems for horizontal alignment across teams executing work—the "How"
- Measures and metrics that have been evolved for the new state of remote working and underpinned by data analysis—the "What"

- Risks, issues, progress, sequencing, and dependencies for governance and delivery
- Team and people information for engagement, cultural norms, and health
- Continuous Improvement, planning, and execution

The degree of granularity required for any of these information streams (or the focus given to each stream per Mado) will vary depending on the needs of the teams. For example, enterprise strategy metrics versus team performance.

There are no two identical organizations and, in turn, no two identical Virtual Obeyas. What each organization does with their Obeya—the ways in which they organize, prioritize, and emphasize their data, culture, processes, and strategies—will depend on which aspects of the business they value, which they feel confident in, which they feel need greater structure and support, and so on.

These four Mados, the information they make visible, and the ways in which that information can be used, are not strict rules. What we have provided here are only suggestions, guiding lights that can help you find your way towards better Agile Governance to achieve the results you're after. Your Obeya should reflect your organization, your teams, and your purpose. So, take the time to design your Obeya purposefully and within the context of your ways of working.

Want to learn more? We recommend you head to our friends at Remote:af who have provided us with a free basic version of their Virtual Obeya Design Studio. Use the QR code below to access.

12

Using the Stanchions in the Real World

Exploring the history and methodologies behind the five stanchions of Agile Governance in theory is all well and good, but our model was designed for the real world. To begin applying these learnings to your own organizational governance, we must start with a brief recap of the stanchions and why we use them.

The five stanchions of Agile Governance are the bedrock of human-centric governance. Regardless of whether your organization is agile, traditional, hybrid, or built upon a model we haven't yet named, these stanchions will function as the connective tissue between tools, methods, processes, ways of thinking and communicating, and more.

The first stanchion, Conductive Leadership, helps us shift from mechanistic to humanistic approaches. It asks leaders to guide and support colleagues like a conductor in an orchestra, providing synchronization and alignment without direct control.

The second, Sensible Transparency, aids the speed of information flow. This aids in decision-making and increases trust, without which organizations can't create true agility or achieve success in a VUCA world.

Third, we have Patterns of Work. This stanchion asks us to question the processes, tools, mindsets, and systems used to conduct our work and complete tasks. Good patterns of work can help us to optimize and evolve; bad patterns of work will sink the ship.

Next is Data-Driven Reasoning, which explores how, what, and why we measure in the workplace. What data actually helps improve the ways we work, and how can we collect and process that data to match the speed of change in today's modern business environment?

Last, but absolutely not least, is Humanity as the Cornerstone. This stanchion asks us to toss away mechanistic controls and invest in trust, by making workers the caretakers and captains of good governance.

Put these five stanchions together, and you have a collection of dynamic ideas and questions that can be applied to any workplace or system of governance. However, actually applying them in the real world may seem daunting.

To get you started, let's peel away the curtain and explore how we've applied each of the five stanchions in real-world studies.

Our Clients

We've helped countless clients improve their businesses by examining their governance through the lens of the five stanchions. For the rest of this chapter we'll draw on three of those clients to help illustrate our ways of working, and how you can take these processes and mindsets and apply them to your own governance. The first of these three clients was the government body (for the purposes of this book, we will call them GovCo from here on in). They had begun to digitize many of their services. This initiative had a realistic, multi-year scope and time frame, and the delivery team had adopted many agile principles, including creating a specifically tailored agile way of working.

This new way of working had a proven track record of successful delivery and had earned the backing of the executive team. However, these changes had the side effect of challenging the status quo in terms of how the organization governed the work.

We were brought in primarily to investigate, assess, and advise. Our focus was to examine the ways in which agile was being adopted, and provide assurance that these new ways of working and governing would provide the necessary oversight and controls to meet the expectations of leadership, stakeholders, and government.

The second client we'll be exploring in these examples is a global organization (let's call them InsureCo). We worked with them for over three years, during which time the company in question wanted to better understand the way they identified, triaged, prioritized, and delivered their work. This understanding would help them to transition away from three-year plans and annualized investment slates to more adaptive, agile ways of working.

We were asked to work as both consultants and enablers of work. Our job was to gather and analyze all the information we could pertaining to their governance framework, then use the five stanchions to create an ongoing backlog of improvement initiatives. In turn, this would help our client uplift the way they delivered value to their customers.

Finally, we'll draw upon learnings from our time developing the Remote Agility Framework (Remote:af). In the early days of the COVID-19 pandemic, we were afforded the opportunity to become co-creators of this framework, which allowed us to synthesize and incorporate the thinking we had developed on the five stanchions into a remote context and, in turn, challenge the ubiquity of the model. We'd already been using the stanchions of Agile Governance in several of our engagements (although we were still developing and codifying them), so this was a great opportunity to distribute the elements of our Agile Governance into a new context, while taking the time to research, learn, and educate others on the principles of effective Agile Governance.

The result of our work with the Remote Agility Framework

was that Remote:af incorporates the stanchions in what are called the "Pillars of Remote Governance": transparency, leadership, systems, and information. These are the Stanchions you've previously learned about, but specifically viewed through a remote lens—and after carefully testing, redesigning, and trialing the core patterns that now make up the framework, we found that the stanchions were largely applicable to a remote context as well. We just had to carefully consider the additional factors unique to the remote landscape, which we were able to test and implement quickly thanks to the support of the founders of the Remote:af. They had a vested interest in getting it right, fast. They needed to shift quickly to a remote-friendly way of working or their business wouldn't survive.

We'll now explore the five stanchions from our work on the ground within these three organizations. These engagements will illuminate the five stanchions from different, complementary angles, and demonstrate how they can be practically applied in your own environment.

12.1 Conductive Leadership in the Real World

When working with any of our clients, understanding the state of their leadership was critical to assisting the growth and development of their governance.

In the case of GovCo, part of our initial mandate was to determine whether their existing governance was fit for purpose. Key to this was understanding how leadership functioned in a traditionally constrained, bureaucratic environment. Could we transform their leadership from conservative to open and agile? How would this affect communication and collaboration, or employees and their roles?

Our role centered around conductive leadership and InsureCo shared some similarities with what we were attempting to achieve at GovCo. Creating conductive leadership is primarily about shifting away from traditional management's task-based approaches. We wanted to show leaders at this organization an alternative: how to think about outcomes when providing a problem to solve, giving their teams clarity around constraints and available resources, and working in sync with teams to help solve that problem.

In both organizations, our goal was to help leaders develop the ways in which they led and the systems underpinning their leadership styles.

We started our examination of leadership by breaking down how people made decisions. But examining how decision-making was distributed and managed at GovCo was no small task. We broke it down into three key areas to focus on:

1. Was authority being taken to the work? Were stakeholders and users alike able to give direct feedback to the team, via avenues such as showcases or backlog refinement sessions?

Wherever possible, we helped empower those actually doing the work on the ground, and tightened feedback loops to improve the speed of progress.

2. When we drilled further into feedback loops, we asked: were the rituals and processes in place (like daily scrums and sprints) actually helping to enable adaptive change and accelerate change requests? A large part of this was examining whether the daily standup or its equivalent helped tell the story of what the current project meant to the customer. Storytelling is a vital part of bringing testers along on the journey and helping them build empathy for the customer, thus creating faster, more accurate feedback. Every step we took to integrate this story into daily rituals aided in tightening their feedback loop.

3. We considered User Research, and asked whether it was doing what it said on the tin: was the research being conducted actually resulting in better design, better engagement, and concrete trust in the product between teams and customers, both internal and external? Or were the results of research not being placed in the hands of those who could make those crucial decisions?

Decision-making at InsureCo was no less complex. We found that, although great decisions were being made at a delivery level, they often ended up re-prosecuted at the management level. The appetite to work differently was there, and the executive leadership group was doing everything right in empowering their teams, but the system itself always slammed on the brakes.

This was a severe constraint upon effective work. It prompted us to ask: what other constraints were in effect? By asking teams to share what they perceived as constraints upon their ways of working, we soon learned that it was critical to determine whether these were real or only perceived. It's not uncommon for teams and individuals to run up against real constraints and rationalize them away instead of addressing them. It's just as common for people to hit what they believe is a constraint, but is actually a simple, easily solved miscommunication.

By asking these questions, we found instances where people felt they had no decision-making power or were unable to move forward with projects, but after some investigation found these concerns weren't actually valid. For example, individuals felt they were limited by the status quo, but there was no actual policy in place to prevent them from moving forward. Other constraints were explicit, where we found the need for leaders to step in and give direction to break through boundaries.

What we were quickly learning from both engagements was that clearer, faster communication was at the heart of many leadership issues. This echoed what we discovered when helping build the Remote Agility Framework. Our biggest discovery when taking leadership into a remote framework was that it was crucial for leaders to identify the most important information to amplify and find ways to increase the volume of that message in both synchronous and asynchronous contexts.

Without this focus, critical messages—like which constraints were being felt most keenly at InsureCo, or whether daily scrums were effective at GovCo—were being lost. Leaders were doing their best but their insights or requests for data were being lost. In fact, through our work at Remote:af, we learned that this was having both a mental and physical impact upon the leadership. The move to remote, coupled with a decrease in control over teams thanks to the loss of "management by walking around" or the typical watercooler directional chat, meant that leaders were doing less natural, supportive, conductive leadership, and more thirty-minute meetings. So many in fact that some leaders were booked out with back-to-back meetings, leaving no time to actually reflect upon the data, plan solutions, or execute quick, collegial conversations.

Leaders intended to be more conductive. The frameworks in place simply didn't allow it.

Conductive leadership and leading with intent are parallel, mutually supportive leadership models. When we dug into conductive leadership at GovCo, our first observation was that the *intent* part of intent-based leadership was already present. The problem was that the system was managing and governing itself in a way that ran counter to what the intent required. This was a result of the leadership approach evolving in such a way that it now interfered with the organization achieving its intent.

Ownership and responsibility were also a concern. We examined the processes people followed while working and discovered that while some of those processes were well-defined, others were vague and ill-formed. People were executing processes blindly and taking little responsibility for the outcomes. In fact, end-to-end ownership of processes and outcomes was consistently missing throughout InsureCo.

Ownership of processes at GovCo was no less complex. The CEO and steering committee understood the value of giving their teams control over a backlog prioritized on business value, but some members of the leadership found it difficult to take their hands off the steering wheel. Certain leads would regularly override the decisions of teams, and ask for immediate pivots that provided no real business value. In short, executives had set some broad guide rails for work, yet when it came time to step back and let that work happen, they got itchy fingers. The result: unproductive teams and tangled backlogs.

This mirrored what we were learning at Remote:af. It was becoming increasingly apparent that success in a remote context relied heavily upon leadership setting clear guide rails that allowed people to work without the constant need for approval or direction… and to then step away and trust those guide rails to operate as intended. Working with poorly formed or vague guide rails was a disaster waiting to happen, especially as teams were becoming more distributed due to lockdowns and remote work. The knee-jerk response of some organizations when they lost visual management control was to create *more* guide rails. What we observed was that a smorgasbord of guide rails was much worse for workers than only a few guide rails designed with quality and clarity.

Of course, setting good guide rails is easy to say and harder to do, as we'd seen at InsureCo. Harder still when working entirely via remote.

We found that creating good guide rails in a remote context required purposeful thinking about an organization's decision-making framework and all its nuances, especially the levels of delegation. We also found that clarity was required around what was a guide rail and what was a constraint. Depending on clarity of communication and quality of leadership, there can sometimes be confusion between "Design like this because we're limited by X, Y, and Z" versus "Design like this because it synergizes well with our sibling-team's patterns of working", or even "Design like this because I say so". We needed leaders to draw a clear line between supportive, guiding, conductive guide rails versus constraints—and then make purposeful decisions so that teams could identify, elevate, challenge, or even remove constraints in their path without dismantling the guide rails.

To achieve this, we found that some guide rails could be set centrally and encompass large swathes of the organization. Others could be set locally, to solve local problems. This ensured that

145

nobody was dancing around irrelevant guide rails, people had the maximum freedom possible to work within the set boundaries, and leaders could focus on making sure the guide rails they created were communicated clearly and transparently.

We had an opportunity to apply a lot of this methodology during our work at GovCo and InsureCo. The key difference between the two engagements was that, when working with GovCo, we had the mandate to step in and make these changes directly. In our time at GovCo, our role was to act as consultants and advisors, helping existing leadership become more conductive without assertively steering the direction of teams ourselves.

This meant we couldn't simply step in and begin establishing guide rails, mandating the use of specific leadership processes, or switching up feedback loops to better enable adaptive change. We had to lead the collective horses of leadership to water, but we couldn't force them to drink.

This caused some difficulties when we learned that, among the executive level at GovCo, none had any formal agile training. They had an awareness of agility, and some even acted in ways they believed were agile, such as the previously mentioned pivots or backlog shakeups to match what they believed were immediate customer needs. Some believed that they didn't need to adhere to methodologies, frameworks, or even the five stanchions. They were executives, after all! They had a different understanding of the work, and exercised power accordingly.

This meant that, before we could dig into questions like whether user research was being utilized to its fullest, or whether authority was being taken to the work, we had to begin with foundational training. Back to the basics: agile fundamentals and terminology like stories and sprints.

It's important to flag that an approach like this required trust between us and leadership, which served as an opportunity to model the sort of trust required between leadership and their teams. It also required significant emotional investment from leaders. None of this would have worked as well as it did if they hadn't *wanted* to become great conductive leaders. Thankfully, the investment was already strong, and we were able to demonstrate for them the value of Conductive Leadership as a stanchion of great governance.

While trust at GovCo was strong, things weren't so rosy at InsureCo. They had a strong focus on accountability, which led to a focus on task completion but a lack of trust between leaders and teams. This was the same across different domains throughout the organization. We needed to find a way to take the trust built inside silos and extend it across the company as a whole. This required building cross functional teams focused on solving problems rather than executing tasks to deliver change. The first of these are now launched and working, with more soon to come. It's these teams that provide the vehicle to really drive the shift from accountability to responsibility.

We also helped to build trust in the teams by demonstrating that we were invested in their growth and future success. A critical element of Conductive Leadership is to ensure your team is competent and capable today, tomorrow, and far into the future. That means planning ahead for ongoing or even continuous training and broadening of skills, so teams can stay effective regardless of what the future brings. When we first came to GovCo we heard that their teams were lacking skills and capabilities for the *now*, let alone the future. Teams knew it, and it had an impact upon morale.

We recommended they look at what skills were increasing in relevance and focus—digital, data, and analytical skills—and begin building training into their weekly schedules. This is something we feel is a function of leadership. It should be leaders who examine the overall capabilities of teams, have foresight and vision, and invest accordingly in training opportunities. It's also up to leaders to make sure their teams have appropriate time to let those lessons sink in before a crisis emerges to test them.

To those who ask, "What if we invest in employee training and then they take the skills we paid for to other companies?" We refer them to this (possibly apocryphal) quote from Henry Ford: "The only thing worse than training your employees and having them leave, is not training them and having them stay."

These shifts to effective, conductive, remote leadership have had quantifiable results—not just for our clients, but across the board. During our work with Remote:af we communicated with multiple organizations and found that those implementing good remote leadership processes had increased productivity of their development teams by upwards of 30%, measured by team data. That would be spectacular in any year, let alone during a pandemic. But these organizations were doing it right: leading by increasing trust in their remote teams, setting clear guide rails, and then allowing their employees to tackle problems as they felt best. It turned out that increased flexibility, coupled with feeling trusted and valued by leaders, correlated with better output. Shocking! Which is why we are now baffled by organizations mandating returns to the office—why would you go against all the data demonstrating that hybrid models are better for everyone? That's a whole other story around traditional leadership philosophy, and not for today.

We saw similar growth towards the end of our engagement with both InsureCo and GovCo. In the case of the former, leadership had started to shift conversation away from tactical management and toward strategic leadership. The executive level was asking new and different questions, and the leadership teams were getting access to new data to support different ways of thinking. The executive team has put in place their first Obeya to provide the space for leaders to come together regularly and collaborate on moving forward their critical strategic programs.

When exploring the stanchion of Conductive Leadership in your own organization, there are a thousand places you could begin. Let's simplify that approach down to five key exercises that can help you start working on conductive and effective leadership in a remote context:

1. **Leadership Self-Assessment**: Start off by honestly evaluating your present leadership practices and style. Analyze the way in which your choices are made, how you share information, and how that affects the development of trust among your teams. Determine what needs to be improved to encourage a more conductive and successful leadership style. The results of this self-evaluation will help you identify the areas of your leadership that require improvement.

2. **Establish Clear Guide Rails:** Regardless of the environment you are working in, remote or traditional, look to setting clear guide rails for your teams. Use these guide rails to define the boundaries within which teams can operate, allowing them the autonomy to make decisions without constant approval or micro-management. And remember that clarity around what is a supportive guide rail and what is a constraint is an important step to Conductive Leadership.

3. **Build Trust within the Teams and the Leaders:** Work towards fostering greater trust and collaboration between leadership and teams by focusing on problem-solving and

outcomes rather than just task completion. This shift from accountability to responsibility creates an environment where the people feel empowered and supported in their growth and success.

4. **Prioritize Communication and Feedback Loops:** Look at how you can improve communication and tighten feedback loops to enable adaptive change. Ensure that critical messages are not lost, and insights are properly shared and acted upon. Effective communication is essential for Conductive Leadership, particularly in remote settings where face-to-face interactions are limited.

5. **Invest in Continuous Training and Skills Development:** Ensure your teams have the skills and capabilities needed not only for current work but also for future challenges. Invest in ongoing or continuous training opportunities to keep people effective and prepared for what lies ahead.

By taking these actions you can begin the journey towards Conductive Leadership, creating a more agile, effective, and responsive organization, regardless of whether it is a traditional office or remote environment.

12.2 Sensible Transparency in the Real World

Exploring sensible transparency during our three primary engagements—with GovCo, InsureCo, and while developing the Remote Agility Framework—was a profound demonstration of the value of the five stanchions. Each of these three engagements required us to consider transparency from different angles—the purpose, value, and when it was appropriate and when it was not—but the answers were always found by returning to the foundational principles of sensible transparency through the lens of Remote Governance.

When we first arrived at GovCo and began to break down which parts of their governance were working and which weren't, we reviewed their transparency from a number of perspectives. First, we considered clarity of purpose and intent. This is a critical factor in Agile Governance which can be considered as part of the Conductive Leadership stanchion as much as it can the stanchion of Sensible Transparency.

When observing how this organization managed clarity of purpose and intent, we asked a few key questions: were teams generally operating using a disciplined funnel of work to balance demand? Did they have a function in place to ensure they managed requests in a fashion within their capacity? If not, how could we help them build such a funnel?

Were teams operating with certainty? Did their backlog refinement and replanning sessions give the teams confidence that they were building the right things, or were their backlogs a series of stabs in the dark? Or worse still, were their backlogs being used as dumping grounds for features that never again saw the light of day?

When it came to benefit realization, we asked: who bore the

onus of responsibility? Were Business Owners and the Steering Committee solely accountable for this? Or were there clear links between Product Features and Integration & Business Change, and further links to benefits and objectives, which provided teams with clarity on the needs and outcomes of feature development, and thus distributed the onus for benefit realization? We also examined business and customer input, and how it related to clarity of purpose. Were customers being asked for input, and if so, were their insights actually being used in a practical way to define further work?

We closely examined the role of the Product Owners within GovCo and considered how they aided in, or obstructed, clarity of purpose and intent. Were they working effectively in their roles and helping to build business understanding? Were they correctly aligned to the relevant customer user groups? Or were they operating in traditional ways that isolated them from customer feedback and needs—a mere changing of the guard from a Business Analyst to a Product Owner in name only?

Finally, we considered whether strategic intent was properly linked to delivery via goal setting. This could be done through OKRs (Objectives and Key Results[76]) or any other methodology, so long as clarity was in place regarding what was being done, and how it related to larger strategies.

Our questions when arriving at InsureCo were similar. We needed to understand why value wasn't being realized, and to what extent that was due to a lack of transparency (or, in some cases, over-transparency leading to confused strategic intent). To what extent was this affecting business understanding? Were teams sharing information and collaborating appropriately, or was silo

---

[76] The essential text on OKRs is Doerr, J.E. (2018). *Measure what matters: OKRs, the simple idea that drives 10x growth.* Great Britain Portfolio.

thinking the law of the land?

We explored, knocked on doors, gathered data, and found some interesting patterns. One piece of feedback that consistently cropped up across InsureCo was that collaboration was far lower than they would've liked. The systems in place necessary for collaboration were foggy and poorly designed, limiting the flow of work between teams. This was, we discovered, an inherited feature of the system rather than an emergent aspect. In essence, prior leadership had created these barriers by design. But why? It's likely that these barriers evolved to solve different problems in a different time, but the data on delivery and performance proved that things needed to change. We needed cross-domain execution to create a fresh, coherent strategy. In fact, the nature of what needed to be changed, the change demand, required coordination between what were supposed to be independent domains. This meant increased collaboration and an organization that better understood itself.

Increased collaboration was also a priority at GovCo. We soon found a key obstacle to achieving this related to transparency: the opaqueness of key documentation.

Prior to our arrival, teams kept their documentation close to their chests. The status of projects was cloudy. At best, other teams or silos could tell whether projects outside their purview were green, amber, or red. This made it difficult to understand which initiatives were dependent upon others, which outcomes were in stasis pending certain data, and so on.

We decided to focus on visualization over documentation. We pressed for teams to convert or refactor complex documents, processes, and data into immediately accessible formats. This had the effect of democratizing key information and making it clearer to all how capabilities were connected i.e. which projects would provide which benefits to which teams. It also shifted leadership thinking from project completion to a more nuanced understanding of growth. They began asking, what capability do we have today that we didn't have yesterday? How do these visualizations demonstrate an unblocking of processes or a maturation of our pipelines?

Those on the executive level found this new approach refreshing. Instead of being forced to sit through meetings and absorb Gantt chart after Gantt chart, they could quickly and easily understand overall progress on a more relevant, human level. It also helped that they were no longer engaging with "garbage" data. Transparency did not mean sharing everything. Instead, with the focus on value creation, the process of data sharing accelerated.

At the time we concluded our engagement with GovCo, we had yet to see a significant business benefit that could be directly credited to this change in how data was visualized and shared. What was more apparent was a change in focus away from traditional metrics and lagging measures like ROI, and towards capabilities and enablement.

Visualization over documentation and the democratization of key, relevant data harkens back to the creation of an Obeya. Bringing people, data, and ideas together into a single space to improve transparency and communication is a parallel process to making that data legible and accessible. At Remote:af, we spent considerable time developing the concept and function of a Virtual Obeya, applying much of what we learned to our time at both GovCo and InsureCo.

What we quickly learned from applying these theories in practice was that the creation of a Virtual Obeya was not just a nice-to-have, but a necessity. In fact, we would argue it is impossible to operate remote Agile Governance without a Virtual Obeya.

Allow us to go one step further. Given the hybrid world we are now living in, where many knowledge workers are privileged to be able to work from home for a large portion of their time, we posit that *all* teams now need a Virtual Obeya of some kind. The shift from obscure documentation to accessible visualization at GovCo would have been a half-measure if we hadn't also enabled the creation of a space where those visualizations could be shared, discussed, debated, and acted upon. So, too, for InsureCo—creating cross-domain execution required a digital space for cross-domain interaction, communication, collaboration, and partnership.

Building this space at InsureCo allowed us to bring people, processes and data together, which in turn allowed us to examine their sensible transparency through the lens of the flow of work. We asked: how visible is their work, really? We were concerned that, without the ability to quickly understand the status of initiatives or change vehicles inside the system, it would be difficult for leaders and teams to prioritize effectively.

We soon discovered that InsureCo was doing some things right. They had good foundational capabilities in place, but with varying levels of adoption and maturity. What this means in practice was that some parts of the organization were working very effectively, using modern workflow management tools to make their work highly visible and transparent. Others were using plans and processes developed in PowerPoint or tracking progress in private excel sheets.

It was critical to get these teams aligned on their methods of visibility, and fast. It was impossible to identify how work moved through the system unless everyone was sharing their flows and constraints in the same manner. We got the teams working to the same methods and using the same tools, then used that information to clarify bottlenecks in the work and identify areas in need of elevation.

Getting all the teams working with the same workflow system and work decomposition approach exposed another imbalance in the system. What we observed was that, when one part of the business added demand that outstripped supply, the actual delivery of change became inequitably distributed. Demand created constraints, which acted as a tourniquet around both delivery and change. What we did to address this was to map flow around the organization and create a clear infographic that exposed where change was happening, and why it was being forcibly limited in other areas. Creating clear links between the constraints, the change, and the impacts of those limitations helped tell a story about the importance of the change: why we were proposing it, what it would achieve, and how it could be done.

We should note that these maps were a select subset of data—the most relevant data, and the most likely to create value. Not all data was shared during this process. The same occurred during our time at GovCo as part of the shift towards visualization. We wanted to increase sharing, but what we termed "garbage" data was excluded, to allow a tighter focus on relevant information regarding capabilities and enablement.

This comes with a corollary: there isn't really such a thing as garbage data. All data is useful somewhere and to someone. We simply encouraged executives, leadership, and teams to bring capabilities and outcome-centric data to the forefront.

However, by excluding or minimizing some forms of data, we ran the risk of damaging trust. It's critical to understand that if you tell teams you're excluding certain data for an important reason, they'll generally believe and agree with your decision. If you simply refuse to share it, then their confidence will be shaken.

That's why we recommend that (as we did during our engagement at GovCo) if data must be restricted or excluded for any reason, the thinking behind that decision be articulated. In our case, it was because we had spoken with stakeholders and understood what data mattered most to them: capabilities, outcomes, and maturation. Had they asked for return on investment, we may have approached the data differently.

When this need is properly articulated, thinking amongst teams and leadership evolves as well. When data on the growth of capabilities and business benefits becomes transparent, the conversation among steering committees changes as well. Governance and strategy adapt to suit, and the entire organization will, over time, organically shift to focus on more valuable metrics.

Strategy was also a concern during our time at InsureCo. We went hunting for strategy… At least, we tried to. The problem was, we couldn't find it. What little strategy existed wasn't being adequately decomposed across the teams, which meant leaders struggled to establish clarity of focus. In fact, there were multiple strategies, all adding to the confusion and the fog of business.

To improve this, we drew upon our work at Remote:af developing the stanchion of Sensible Transparency. We found there was a clear link between achieving transparency of progress, dependencies, and impediments, and the length, quality, and dynamism of planning and strategy. To summarize, short-cycle planning enables transparency, while quarterly, big-room planning impedes it. The more remote the organization, the more critical it is to utilize short-cycle planning in order to enable transparency and adaptability. Short-cycle planning also helps organizations mimic the cadence of real-world events, which require strategic adaptation on an ever-accelerating basis. Major change is occurring in our world every three to four months—if planning and strategy can't keep pace, an organization will falter.

We took this into practice at InsureCo and used a Virtual Obeya to draw both people and information into a space where planning and strategy could accelerate. Since then, large changes have been put into place. A single, unifying strategy has been established, guiding the teams and prioritization of work. This also allowed for the creation of a well-planned three-year roadmap to scaffold and support short-cycle planning, increasing the clarity around strategic decisions. These changes have allowed for huge improvements in how the organization prioritizes and aligns people and resources. As a result, the teams are now able to get greater value out of their limited capacity.

To wrap up, we have some final observations and commonalities across these case studies related to the stanchion of Sensible Transparency. These two specific actions have huge potential to improve transparency of work and enable better decision-making.

1. **Adopt standardized workflow tooling**. Specifically, we asked every team at InsureCo, involved in change delivery, to run and manage that change through the same workflow management application. In the case of InsureCo, this involved the co-creation of workflow states, the decomposition of the process throughout the organization, and then the migration of over seventy delivery teams from old practices to new. The result was work visibility increasing from as low as 5% to as high as 30% in the space of a few months, with more improvements coming down the pipeline, and within a year getting closer to 70%. Getting core teams established with the same workflow management application has also allowed us to switch focus towards more intensive adoption and optimization, as well as further connection across the delivery value chain. This allows us to trace our work at any point in the system, and to have the work visible to any team or leader.

2. **Adopt digital whiteboarding for communication and clarity**. This practice emerged during lockdown and has exploded from the bottom-up due to its wide applicability

and ease of use. The utility of the whiteboard application (in our case, Miro) has been proven many times over, at both InsureCo and GovCO, to the extent that they are now onboarding it as a standard Enterprise tool. They're also looking for ways to integrate it into the workflow management applications. This, coupled with the advent and integration of work-accelerating AI tools, has helped to support and scaffold the creation of work within the system.

Combined, all the processes, tools and ways of thinking discussed in this chapter have worked to improve Sensible Transparency in the real world, strengthening one of the five stanchions.

If your next question is, "How do I dig into Sensible Transparency in my own company?", we have five key exercises to get you started.

1. **Canvas the system:** Always start from where you are. It's a common truism in kanban adoption that you start with where the work and what the flow of the work is today, and you mature from there. It's always been that you commence work with an understanding of the current state, the as is. Get to know how the organization works and develop that starting position.

2. **Find the data:** One thing that most modern organizations are not sure of is the data. The challenge is both finding it and making it useful enough to support decision-making in a timely manner. Find the people in your organization who are focused on performance and have a passion for finding and using data; they are always there somewhere and their nuggets of insight will help craft the whole. Gather as much

relevant information as possible to craft your starting points. You also need to make decisions on how much transparency is the right amount. Transparency comes with a cost; nothing can be fully open without losing value. Put the limits in place.

3. **Agree on the tooling:** It's not much use having access to the information for decision-making if people can't find or maintain it. Pick the right presentation layers for your organization so that you can create meaningful, accessible dashboards for reporting and decision-making. Stabilize that across the organization.

4. **Elevate the information:** This is where tools such as **Virtual** Obeya, Power BI, and the like used for visualization, come into their own. Start putting out information and using it when talking to the work. You can get stuck in analysis paralysis forever. There needs to be a point where you have enough confidence that your information is directionally correct—if not 100% perfect—and enough to drive conversations. Often, your data will challenge opinions and perspectives, sometimes power bases and control, so the sooner you start doing that, the faster your transformation will be. Don't be afraid to move forward, take the feedback and adjust—often it requires just a little bravery and challenging the status quo.

5. **Improve:** The world doesn't stand still and neither does your information—the way you gather it, or the best way to present it. Any system depreciates over time, it entrophies, unless you constantly inspect and adapt and introduce new energy and things. You need to implement the mechanisms

supporting and enabling constant improvement and refinement, as well as data quality and governance, or the usability of your information will degrade. This need to reflect and improve is the core of agility and often gets forgotten.

The key in a VUCA world is speed of information flow, which allows speed of decision-making and response time. The old world, where people often used information to create control and power, essentially to survive within particular environments, is no longer practical at the pace of the world today. The days of intrigue and gossip mongering at court are long gone. By opening up your information, where it's practical and legal to do so, you empower people to focus on the right information, which allows for better decision-making in the long run. It's a key pillar of how you better govern your work.

12.3 Patterns of Work in the Real World

When we developed and implemented key findings from the Patterns of Work stanchion across these three clients, we found a number of similarities that strengthened our theories and helped flesh out what it meant to create strong Patterns of Work in remote, asynchronous environments.

We began with GovCo, where observing and understanding patterns of work was critical. We had been asked to help their teams develop and evolve their ways of working, and their leadership—as well as the Government body—needed assurance that the newly adopted ways of working would still meet standards and expectations, providing the public with the same, or better, quality of outcome that they were used to. Public Service is generally held to a more controlled approach to project execution than many private sector organizations.

The teams at the center of the transformation had already made use of the Organizations Change Model. Their personal, bespoke model was well documented, and included clear information on what was required to transition between different working states. The leadership group had specifically crafted a pattern of work that not only allowed for successful application of their objectives but could meet public service standards.

This had helped them to establish an operating rhythm that was effective inside their own team, but it was having unexpected impacts on other teams throughout the organization. This was partly due to unaligned working practices and cadences, which further impacted business operations. In addition, it created noise in the system thanks to an emergent "us versus them" culture that needed to be remediated. This is also a pattern we see a lot—where the "new" ways of the working team are challenging the system and doing things differently, getting more attention from the organization.

Understanding patterns of work was no less critical at InsureCo. If we wanted to understand how their work was executed, we needed to examine and understand the pattern in which work flowed from the idea holder to the idea executor, as well as how long that took. Conceptualizing that entire process was key... although, it's more accurate to say processes, plural. *Everything* is a process in the modern work environment. This is another core to agility that gets forgotten or dismissed—the need to create clarity of your ways of working as a process that you can work to, and also develop interactions with others.

Some processes are large while some are extremely brief. Some processes are clearly defined and managed, they are consistent and repeatable. They are executed without drama. These are ideal homes for things such as robotic process automation. Other processes are more unclear, emergent, and volatile. These inconsistencies are often a reaction to the work being done and can't necessarily be ironed out of the process. What we can do is build transparency into the system and map out the flow of those processes, so that the inconsistencies and volatilities are anticipated and understood to the highest degree possible. This also acknowledges that, as scenarios change, so do the processes that require execution. Therefore, as change in process is constant, the adaptability of the system must match.

Teasing out which processes were which was our first step at InsureCo. We did so by undertaking an exercise where we worked through almost thirty different change-adjacent teams and domains, mapping out their flow of work. What we found was that nearly thirty different value streams had been defined to move work from the backlog to done. Some of those streams were well-defined and meticulously planned, with continuous improvement as a key part of their thinking. While others were a collection of post-its where people mapped out what they *thought* they were achieving from day to day. These teams naturally had inconsistent processes and weren't really following the procedures required to achieve positive change. And often we found a defined process that wasn't actually what teams were doing!

Our observations corresponded with what we'd heard from teams and leaders within the system: that inconsistency and lack of clarity was making it hard to get things done, especially trying to achieve an outcome that spanned systems and domains and included incongruous ways of working.

So, how could we create consistency?

For this, we turned to our work with Remote:af. The Remote Agility Framework considers Patterns of Work through the lens of Systems. In our time at Remote:af, we considered how a broad move to remote ways of working turned effective digital environments and systems from nice-to-haves into necessities for workplace success. None of this sounds radical with the lockdown years well behind us, but at the time, getting a handle on these concepts was the emergent problem most urgently in need of solving.

What we determined was that the exact tools mattered less than finding systems that enabled the operation of effective virtual workplaces. Virtual collaborative tools, whiteboards, conferencing and sharing were all essential, but what was critical was considering how well these enabled and supported patterns of work in the new paradigm rather than trying to replicate the physical, in-person experience.

It's no surprise that some of the largest growth in the technology sector during the pandemic years was amongst organizations that provided remote work equipment and solutions: Miro, Slack, Atlassian, AWS, Microsoft, and so on. As they say, the secret to getting rich in a gold rush is selling picks to the miners.

We took our learnings regarding tools and systems from Remote:af and used them to fuel improvements at InsureCo. We asked, what digital environments and systems are critical here? Which tools suit existing ways of working, and which will elevate processes? What fundamental changes to teams could support this push towards consistency?

We'll return to InsureCo in a moment and discuss what changes were implemented. First, we'd like to briefly discuss how consistency, and codified ways of working, were also critical at GovCo. We needed to work with teams inside this client organization to examine their ways of working, and ensure they were codified in a clear, accessible manner that gave team employees confidence and an ultimate source of truth to refer to when things got foggy. We asked whether work had been documented in a single place managed by the teams, for example: Jira, Confluence, or Github.

We also considered how work was broken down. Was there a standardized breakdown structure in place that was followed across the board in a disciplined manner, or was it more ad hoc? If the latter, how could we assist in codifying those breakdown structures? This extended to Epics and Stories: did they have defined structures and naming conventions? Where could friction points be eased by making everything a little more structured?

Continuous Integration & Continuous Delivery (CI/CD) also fell under the umbrella of ways of working. Did teams have full use of CI/CD automation, including testing with stated coverage? When tests took place, were there automated tests in place with clearly stated coverage of base code? If not, why? We also considered inter-team and cross-team communication. Was there a single, agreed-upon method of communicating between dependent teams? If not, could we help establish one? In addition, did teams share a single, well-developed, up-to-date roadmap that encompassed the evolution of the product?

We left GovCo to sit with these questions and find solutions that brought teams together with unified, coherent, consistent Patterns of Work, rather than piecemeal, team-by-team solutions.

Returning to our engagement with InsureCo, we needed to get a little more hands-on. To solve the problems we observed within the Patterns of Work stanchion, we constructed two key activities:

1. To create more enduring teams and move away from project centered approaches that traditionally take people to new work, rather than take work to stable teams. This means designing and implementing around the principles of flow, as well as creating observable designs, processes, and patterns that allow multiple teams to connect and sync into a team of teams. This allows them to connect into problems to be solved. At InsureCo, the first of these long-lived teams has been designed and launched. Others are going through ideation now. We use a consistent approach to design and launch these teams, which allows us to align future teams on ways of working and replicable patterns. Much of this work was based upon the foundation provided by the Remote Agility Framework, although we have made tweaks and adjustments where necessary to suit the constraints of the organization.

2. To create opportunities for more aligned ways of working and practices by standardizing the workflow management application adoption for workflow traceability. Yes, we know that these methods have limits upon the number of permitted workflow states and items. This, in turn, puts constraints on teams. However, the teams are then left to

decide how to work at their own discretion, using these constraints as enabling boundaries. What follows is greater alignment across teams regarding patterns and practices. The result is that when people move between teams, they're shifting into familiar environments. Dependencies are also clearer, work is more traceable end-to-end, and capabilities are uplifted. In short, standardization of DevOps gives workers power and flexibility, and uplifts collaboration in multi-domain, complex, and complicated problems. This can often be a challenge in a fragmented organization as every team's scenario is unique, like a snowflake. Yet this is a critical step to digitizing clarity of work.

These two smaller goals fed into our larger goal: to help InsureCo create and maintain a level of alignment and consistency within the Patterns of Work stanchion. Every function within this stanchion needed to be clear as to the way it worked and operated, so that when projects and work spanned boundaries or teams, there were strong anchors in place that teams could use as a foundation for communication and collaboration. Small limitations imposed at the team level created an abundance of flexibility at the Strategic Enterprise level.

One could argue the merits of this trade-off. In some organizations of different sizes and structures, this might not be the right call for their Patterns of Work. For our client, it was exactly what they needed. None of their teams were islands and were driven largely by the architecture of their software systems (as we so often see, communication channels driving solutions—thanks again Conway)[77]. They had to internalize and be guided by that knowledge.

All our efforts creating consistency are supported by the work we did at Remote:af, which reinforced how crucial it is to codify how work is done… particularly when it is being done asynchronously. That was where the strength of the Remote Agility Framework demonstrated itself, especially with the stanchions of Agile Governance as a core, stabilizing anchor. When we say codification, we mean workflow design, such as value stream management and mapping.

What we found interesting in our time with Remote:af was that, when speaking with multiple partner companies, we found that this codification process was generally recognized as important—even in the context of onsite teams—but it wasn't being done nearly enough. Especially when it came to onsite teams. It was only with the forcible move to remote work that many organizations had the catalyst to accelerate activities like using value stream mapping to define flows of work. As we've seen many times before, sometimes good ideas require a nudge before they find their footing. As a result of so many organizations diving into these processes, we now consider value stream mapping, and similar activities, mandatory in any team aiming to deliver collaboratively.

Consistent Patterns of Work at both GovCo and InsureCo were key to their success. However, the journey towards excellence at GovCo wasn't quite done. When we concluded our engagement, their teams and leaders had a number of questions to explore internally, and to use as springboards for further growth.

For example, we examined ways of working as they pertained to customer interactions. Did developers and testers alike interact

---

[77] "Organizations, who design systems, are constrained to produce designs which are copies of the communication structures of these organizations." Often referred to as "Conway's Law" – Melvin Conway, 1967

directly with the customer, both in relation to User Acceptance Testing and Post Verification Testing? When they developed the user experience, were they working side by side with the customer? Were they giving that user experience the focus it deserved?

We engaged in Systems Reflection: the process of examining the system as a whole and understanding how it works, why it works, and what dysfunctions may arise over time as a result of the shape or function of the system. When we engaged with GovCo, we asked questions like: is there evidence of strong technical engineering practices and tooling? Do these practices provide a proper foundation for agility, and do they work to increase the quality and reduce the risk of releases? Are software release practices tight and working to a consistent cadence? In addition, who owns those practices? Was ownership concentrated in a single team, or role, or did they have joint ownership across the technical and business arms of the organization?

We also asked how employees were contracted in their current positions. Are they permanent employees? Part time? Contracted? Consultants? And so on. We needed to know if a majority of the teams, particularly those in key roles, were permanent employees. This impacts who holds the inherent IP of the system, and the stability of systems long-term. Overweighting to contingent or consulting type engagements leads to loss of IP and long-term indirect cost, yet alone being more expensive generally.

Leaders at GovCo used the work we initiated to build upon these questions after we concluded our engagement.

Of all the questions we left GovCo to consider, the cadence of delivery was one of the most important. Our work at Remote:af demonstrated that delivery and planning is performed in increasingly shorter cadences—even shorter than the rapid cadences many traditional Agilists are used to—in order to enable expedient adaptation and decisioning. This is a necessary move in situations where the domain is constantly shifting and VUCA is at work inside and out. All teams run the risk of making mistakes or bad decisions, but by empowering remote teams to build bespoke, highly efficient patterns of work, they run the risk of building upon bad decision after bad decision and ending up off track long before the misalignment is noticed.

Instead, all evidence now points to the benefits of shortening cadences and ensuring that alignment to the global strategy is a part of every cadence. This allows remote teams to confirm the right priorities are being worked on, without time lag increasing risk and cost of delay in the unfortunate scenario that they're headed down the wrong path.

As a result of these learnings, we've prioritized the increased cadence of delivery and planning for future engagements, and as a core component of the Patterns of Work stanchion.

When you're first looking into Patterns of Work inside your own organization, there are countless ways to begin. Our top five recommendations for getting started are:

1. **Map the current flow:** The start point is knowing how work gets to done in your system today. There are a variety of approaches or methods that can be used to achieve this— Value Stream Mapping, SIPOC mapping, Systems Thinking Approach for Implementing Kanban, and so on. Gather all current known process flows, synthesize them, and create the most meaningful representation of how work moves from idea to done—the life cycle of change. It's always critical to capture as much of the current way of working as possible to baseline the future. Respect what is already there, and the work done by others, to optimize and improve. The fastest path to failure is trying to design external to the system and then forcing that new way of working onto your

teams. By mapping the current state, you bring people along on the journey of change by visualizing issues in their current workflow and removing opinion.

2. **Select constraints and design new patterns:** There are constraints in any system of work, some are enabling and some preventative, some you can challenge, and some can't be changed. Clarifying what these are, and their nature, will allow you to tackle the problems that can be solved. Elevate them to leadership so that they know what you're going after and can support by removing impediments to change. There is no point designing a future state operating model and flow of work if there are immovable constraints that prevent the model from being successful. You can then use these as core principles for designing the new patterns of work. Ensure your proposed design has multiple approaches and patterns for different problem domains, as you need to allow for variability where teams are solving different things in different contexts. Pick the common pillars and make them fixed, enabling constraints, and be clear on what can be variable.

3. **Pick the domains and problems to prioritize:** Now that you have your patterns of work you need to pick the domains or areas to prioritize. Don't try to tackle the whole organization, pick the areas where you can challenge the system and have willing teams to work with. You might find this referred to as a Coalition of the Willing… rather than cooperation of the impacted. You also want to find one that has enough complexity to it because if you pick a simple area to tackle then you might not learn enough to be successful. It often works best to start with two or three

specific areas and move them forward in parallel. After all, being able to demonstrate progress remains vital to continued support for any change efforts.

4. **Develop the change plan and transition teams incrementally and safely:** Ensure that you have a strong change management plan that supports the outcome, and the steps people need to take to get there. You also need to ensure that the teams you're working with are able to dedicate capacity to shift their way of working, otherwise this becomes an "and" to their day job. One of the most important things a team should do is design and improve their ways of working. We often don't give them the space to do this. After all, if you're not improving processes then you're actually going backwards as the system progresses around you. Then you end up needing large-scale transformation because you haven't kept pace.

5. **Reflect and improve:** The last key element is ensuring that you learn from the process of transformation and transition, adapting your approach so it is always relevant and improving. This extends to the teams: giving them the space, tooling, capacity, and capability to improve their own ways of working. Give them the guide rails and ability to decide the how, which will promote ownership and ensure continuous improvement towards maintaining productivity. Many agilists will forget that being human centric and moving Patterns of Work towards being more agile will create a more empowered Workforce but still needs to be productive and efficient. Part of reflecting on the work means constantly demonstrating that the system is getting better.

The way teams work is fundamental to not just governing the system, but getting the best out of our agile teams. We often hear the throwaway line that an organization's ways of working are not fit for purpose, but it's rare to find the corresponding approaches and solutions being enabled to solve for that. Many organizations are also provided glossy proposals by consultancies that suggest changing the ways of working is all that is needed to solve all an organization's problems. Both approaches are incorrect. Finding the right ways of working for your organization is critical, yet they also need to be reflective of the system today and the environment in which work happens. The best outcome is to design collaboratively, purposely, and consistently, and enable your teams to take as much of that responsibility as you can safely delegate within the clear constraints you need to maintain.

12.4 Data-Driven Reasoning in the Real World

The foundation of the Data-Driven Reasoning stanchion is formed from metrics and measuring. Whether it was in our work with GovCo, InsureCo, or our work with Remote:af developing the pillars of Remote Governance, everything began with and revolved around the collection and analysis of relevant metrics. When we began our work with GovCo, we knew we had to completely understand how they gathered their metrics and measures, and how they used that information, if we wanted to help them improve the use of data in their governance. We started by asking questions of leaders and teams, such as: what are the standard metrics and measures being used inside this system? Are standard agile metrics like committed vs delivered, velocity, cumulative flow, and sprint goals being effectively employed? Are flow-based metrics used to measure the lead, cycle, and wait times of work progressing through the system?

Just as important to the collection of metrics was how they were being used. Were those metrics being used to baseline and improve teams, and if so, then how? We investigated whether these metrics were utilized for real-time reporting. Was there transparency of real-time progress across areas such as dependencies, risks, issues, impediments, and initiatives?

The information we gathered provided several potential outcomes to leadership, as well as various stakeholders, participants in the system of work, and the teams themselves. The primary outcome was to validate that the teams were using well-defined practice to gather data and using that to inform decision-making. As these teams were each using bespoke ways of working, they were producing unique data that couldn't be measured against any single, central Gantt Chart or Excel spreadsheet. As such, teams were individually validating that they were using the right data, in the right way, at the right time, and for the right decisions. Thankfully, those teams rose to the challenge and demonstrated this handily. Another key outcome from the questions and review was that other participants now trusted the system to deliver to the change demand, and that they could now better align dependencies across a wide variety of teams.

We didn't have to hunt for data quite so hard when we began working with InsureCo. In fact, when we walked through their doors and started talking about the stanchion of Data-Driven Reasoning, they assured us that they loved data. *Loved* it.

Here's the thing: every organization says that they love data and make data-driven decisions. And that's probably true for financial decisions. Maybe even investment and customer directional decisions too. But the claim gets wobbly when we move to other areas. For example, how often do you hear of data being used for decisions related to internal performance measures? Sometimes. Not nearly as often as finance, where we tend to overweight data for reporting and underweight it for tactical and strategic management decisions.

When we commenced our work with InsureCo, we were assured that the workflow was improving. Speeding up, in fact. But we needed to verify this to make sure we were getting the right data to answer the right questions. We started by hunting for data on how the system was performing at that time, versus where they wanted the system to eventually be. We also needed that data to properly understand what to measure improvement against.

We quickly discovered that the client had already made some positive progress. Valuable work had gone into trying to manage the flow of initiatives at a basic level. This served as a useful launchpad for understanding the system as a whole and any preconceptions around how the system functioned (or failed to function). This overview of initiatives included a manually operated Change Backlog that was standalone from the larger system and being managed by private individuals. Even so, it provided fascinating insights into core elements including lead time, throughput, wait times, and delays.

We quickly learned that, counter to the narrative that everything was going smoothly, processes were not functioning as intended. Lead times were well above industry averages, and getting worse as more demand was being placed on the system. More work was coming in, and less was getting out. This was both perceived and felt, but not agreed to or elevated.

It was an interesting lesson in the usefulness of data that could otherwise be overlooked. The source of the data wasn't pristine, or completely reliable, but in aggregate it demonstrated important trends validating our theory that work was slowing down, rather than speeding up. These insights provided a baseline of information for the remainder of the work that we both measured and improved against.

As always, data trumped opinion. That observation has been proven true time and time again, and our work at Remote:af only reinforced this. For clarity, the stanchion of Data-Driven Reasoning is paralleled by the Information pillar in the Remote Agility Framework. As we worked with Remote:af to develop the concepts that would become their pillars and our stanchions, we quickly learned it was essential to ensure systems inside organizations were being reflected digitally, and that they were generating sufficient data to make informed decisions. Without this data being created, shared, and consumed via a Virtual Obeya, it was near impossible to enable effective leadership and cross-organizational transparency, meaning opinion would usually take precedence over data.

It was readily apparent to us that some of the most important information was team and individual health metrics, which provided insights into their well-being. With the switch to remote ways of working, these became even more important, as leaders were missing out on the traditional water-cooler chats and checkups. However, many high-performing teams in surveyed organizations had already reached similar conclusions organically; they knew the value of maintaining a lens into their internal performance and team health. Many other organizations, though, are only now crossing the chasm[78] (to borrow a phrase from Geoffrey Moore) and seeking deeper insights into team health.

We see this all too often. We've visited so many organizations that talk about being data-led and data-driven, with a plethora of KPIs and targets to present, but flounder once we dig deeper. It's disappointing discovering that an organization is ignorant to its own flow and performance, outside of any data not directly related to financials. It's rare to work with an organization that doesn't care in some way for team health—but as per Deming,[79] they can't improve what they can't measure.

In some cases, the introduction of data-driven decisioning is not easily accepted due to the learned behaviors and culture of the organization having served them well in traditional delivery. The introduction of data-driven decisioning is sometimes difficult to embrace. One such instance involved the introduction of agility within GovCo where agile processes and governance methods brought about new techniques for the production, sourcing, and consumption of data. Additionally, it brought contention.

Real-time data rollups were built by the agile program to

[78] Moore, G.A. (2014). Crossing the Chasm: Marketing and Selling Disruptive Products to Mainstream Customers. 3rd ed. New York: Collins Business Essentials.
[79] Dr Edwards Deming: The New Economics – 14 Points for Management; Out of The Crisis (MIT Press) (pp. 23-24)https://deming.org/explore/fourteen-points

facilitate quick decision-making. Workflow data was used to demonstrate progress and highlight dependencies, risks, and roadblocks. This was extended to the point of developing real-time dashboards that displayed metrics for success, construction information, and defect resolution.

GovCo challenged the traditional methods of governance used for reporting and approval, such as document trails, signoffs, and registers. A good example is that, like many organizations, progress toward delivering the software required a visit to the Change Advisory Board (CAB) (along with a plethora of signed and sealed documents). The CAB operated on a quarterly delivery cycle, as most releases in the organization followed a very traditional waterfall cycle.

This group had established CICD pipelines and practices (continuous integration, continuous delivery, and continuous deployment), as well as a very strong automated testing program. They used this capability to deliver to internal environments. However, while their business representatives had been brought along and were familiar with the new reporting dashboards, this did not extend to production, or a shortening of the delivery timelines for production.

After we'd spent some time working with GovCo, we suggested that the digital reporting and release dashboards be incorporated into the governance cycle, replacing the paper trails while allowing for discussions and enquiries about quality and due diligence. It was deemed acceptable to lower the release cycle to monthly and make digital sign-off against any variations to the norm.

The key factor here was not just challenging the current process head-on. It was education, which in turn provided data to promote understanding and recognition that expedient and accurate decisions could be made using the new methods. This also ensured that audit, risk, and compliance information was included for a release cycle to ensure that it fell within their risk tolerance, while still enabling teams to deliver faster.

Something we found interesting while developing the Data-Driven Reasoning stanchion at InsureCo was that the elevation and transparency of data had the potential to create contention and conflict. There was a misconception that some parts of the delivery system that had been over-invested in were actually performing to expectations, even though all the evidence found in lead time and quality-type metrics contradicted that assumption.

Some key areas were also reluctant to embrace the data of workflow and performance, preferring to focus on traditional metrics. Although there was a desire to gather and publish data that would be accessible for all, there was a developed behavior (perhaps even an internal culture) where any information that could be perceived as negative would be held back until the message could be managed. This practice clashes with our fast-paced, data-driven world. The problem to be solved moves too quickly, and the ramifications of a lack of transparency are increasingly profound.

More system conflict was caused by the visualization of demand exceeding supply and that by constantly starting work we were in fact slowing down outputs. The decision to begin "stopping" work had far-reaching consequences with the potential to impact outcomes and plans made the year before. The fact was that the entire concept of twelve-month fixed plans is outdated in a VUCA world. And this lack of planning flexibility played out when trying to control Work In Progress by not starting on new work until everything in progress was finished. The temporary pain of stopping unnecessary work and adjusting outdated plans was critical to getting this system conflict under control. Finally, the elevation of KPIs when using data (especially where those KPIs don't align across functions) caused further conflict, creating an environment where competition was the order of the day for scarce resources. We needed to turn that conflict into collaboration, and alignment on data-driven decisioning was the answer.

We mentioned previously that data can be a double-edged sword (see *Chapter 9 Data-Driven Reasoning*). Here, this was proven true… at least, in the early months of our engagement. It took more than six months for the data to actually become understood, and for people to trust that data when it came time to make critical decisions.

Perhaps part of what finally helped them adjust to and accept the reality of data-driven decisioning was the realization that, just as the data suggested, too much work was being put through the system, and delivery was suffering as a result. This forced leadership to direct their teams to focus and prioritize. It took data to help them realize that they couldn't achieve everything all at once.

There were three key actions we took during this engagement to help establish the case for a switch to a data-driven perspective. These were:

1. To improve, stabilize, and uplift the reliability of data sources. We knew we needed strong, accurate baselines to measure against, and to be using data for reliable decision-making. None of this could be achieved without trusting where the data was coming from. As such, we performed several ongoing sweeps of data sources, checking each element for reliability. We also invested heavily in data and reporting, beginning by using static outputs. Once those outputs were stabilized and reliable, we moved to using Power BI (the Microsoft Reporting suite). This allowed them to dynamically update their data against Power BI reports, providing a clear, accessible dashboard for our core system performance measures. With the dashboard

functioning, everyone had visibility and could use those performance measures to improve efficiency and effectiveness.

2. To create a reliable data source as part of the migration to a single workflow management application. By moving every team into a state where they consistently traced their work in a transparent fashion, we were able to move away from using manual dashboards, and towards a completely automated system that built coherent datasets straight from the source.

3. To present our plans, methods, and achievements in as many places as possible. This meant talking constantly about the data we were collecting and the insights it provided. We began discussing it at an executive level during every quarterly performance review, with the goal of increasing the frequency to a six-week cadence. This isn't just a local domain goal. We consider it a technology goal that will improve efficiency of delivery, as well as identify how much work moves through the system as compared to the first-year baselines.

Evidence is that InsureCo using the agreed and baselined performance measures had, over a six-month period, improved its overall measurable productivity by 6.1%. This is the result of several change initiatives and ongoing continuous improvement work across the system, but without taking the stance that data matters and stabilizing it first, that would not be demonstrable. Needless to say, the executive leadership were pleased with what they were seeing.

That being said, as we collected increasing amounts of data

from Insureco and, in concert with teams and leaders, converted that data into actionable insights, we learned that some of our earlier observations and assumptions were incorrect. This required us to pivot on some of the activities and mental models we used as part of this engagement. We are human, and always going through a journey of learning and improving. However, we'd rather start from strong assumptions and then adapt as the data arrives than wait for a perfect analysis and perfect solution that may never arrive. This reinforces the need to consider Transformation as a series of options to be explored, reserving the right to pivot based on feedback and learning. You can't turn a ship if you're standing still.

Data-Driven Reasoning allows for this type of approach. It reduces the time spent designing the solution, creating more time for you to dive in and do the work.

As we write this book in mid-2023, Remote:af is now being used in organizations across the globe. So too have we seen the adoption of the Remote Governance pillars. We've already seen how effective this framework can be for organizations standing on the front line of the battle against VUCA, and we expect that as learnings continue to roll in, the pillars of Remote Governance will continue to evolve. So too will the five stanchions of Agile Governance. They are both ever-evolving frameworks that we believe will be relevant and effective for decades to come.

To begin building the Data-Driven Reasoning stanchion in your own organization, we recommend you:

1. **Cast your gaze**: Observe what is being used today, and how, and look for opportunities to scale rather than assume you must begin from a zero base. In other words, respect the system you have today and start from where you are.

What are your outcomes and objectives, and how can they be achieved using what you already have at hand?

2. **Define your standards**: Determine what you need to codify and what can be variable. Determine what system you will use, which are the right practices to adopt, where you should store these standards, and how. Do these as collaboratively as possible, and also be ready to move forward when there is enough alignment. Accessibility is key, as is ease of adoption. Keep cost in mind as you determine what will best enable people to work as efficiently and effectively as possible across the delivery ecosystem. Decisions must be made that will extend beyond the initial phase and far into the future.

3. **Support your change journey:** Plan for transition and training, as well as supporting people to move to new systems, standards, and ways of working. Guides, tools, and coaching are important for success. The best endeavors are often not enough—you need to invest to ensure an outcome, or you'll just get faster horses. Plan the change journey out, and communicate excessively.

4. **Baseline your reports**: Once data is established, collected, and used, baseline it and create the reporting suite. Publish, communicate, and update often. Be visible early, accept that your processes will change and you will get things wrong, and be ready to learn from the process of failure through inspecting and adapting. Don't set out to fail, of course. Set out to learn quickly and pivot. Building trust in the data is great, but you also want to build trust in the teams using it,

as well as their belief that the data is fit for purpose. Lack of trust in the outputs is a killer in this phase of transition.

5. **Visualize, communicate, optimize, and improve**: You must now put your money where your mouth is and actually use the data to drive your decision-making. Share it, talk about it, and tell stories about how it's making a difference. Broadcast freely and enthusiastically, but not fanatically. You must still be honest about what your data is achieving and where it's falling short, and you must always look to improve and optimize your processes.

It's interesting how many times we've gone into an organization that hasn't been able to provide or does not know its own performance data. Yet they will gather and report on endless other KPIs and financial metrics and measures. If you don't know your system and you don't know your work then you literally can't improve. At the same time, many of these organizations will have amazing people, doing amazing things, trying to craft these insights. If you do nothing else, find the people who are passionate about these things, help them, and give them the platform to be successful. They will probably solve the data questions for you!

12.5 Humanity as the Cornerstone in the Real World

This brings us to the last stanchion: Humanity.

Before we dive into how we helped our three clients better understand how Humanity could form the cornerstone of great governance, we'd like to first revisit the Heart of Agile, which served as one of our guiding influences while creating this stanchion.

The Heart of Agile—Dr.Alistair Cockburn's model for simplifying and clarifying the most critical imperatives of agility—has been a significant influence on all the Stanchions. It's the Heart of Agile's emphasis on people that has most affected us during our years of working with Alistair as Heart of Agile Guides. And we regularly use this to check or identify whether the work we're doing has the necessary human quotient.

The Heart of Agile orients itself around attitudes and behaviors. It guides us to focus on the fact that no matter what framework you use, collaboration (to wit, humans working together) done well will improve information flow. That flow improves decisions, specifically humans making decisions, and therefore improves delivery. It ensures you remember to take the time to reflect and improve, together, in order to enhance collaboration and delivery.

The longer we worked with Alistair and the Heart of Agile, the clearer it became that humanity was a central tenet of good governance. It couldn't be a nice-to-have appended on to the other stanchions; it needed a stanchion of its own. By making this decision, we ensured that Agile Governance had a clear humanistic focus as opposed to being consumed by the mechanistic processes that traditional governance so ritualistically puts in place to control or command. This mirrors what Heart of Agile teams set out to do. That ethos is at the center of what we are trying to do.

Many of our theories on implementing Humanity as the Cornerstone remained theories until, much like the preceding four Stanchions, we had the opportunity to implement our findings in our engagements. When we did so, we found similarities that strengthened the model and helped flesh out our understanding of what it meant to curate and create meaningful human connections in remote, asynchronous environments. People are people, and despite much of our business moving en masse to remote, many of the challenges of the physical world continued to manifest in the digital (or, in some cases, grow exponentially). As Andrew Blain from Remote:af would say, "In remote contexts, silos become chasms".

So, let's explore some of the questions we explored with those three clients, and how they changed their lenses on Humanity as the Cornerstone of good governance.

First, let's talk about GovCo. We began our engagement by peeling back the lid on their internal culture to find out where things were working well, and where they weren't. This began with a dive into trust and transparency.

We asked questions about safety, such as: did employees feel the organization was psychologically safe; that they were able to raise issues or share failures as learnings without fear of repercussion? In the same vein, was trust evident inside teams or was there an undercurrent of blame running throughout the internal culture?

We also wanted to know whether teams had built trusted relationships both internally and externally. Could people have candid conversations with other employees outside of their immediate circles? If issues occurred, did they feel able and safe in raising those issues with colleagues and leaders?

Transparency also figured into our discussions on culture. We needed to know whether transparency was broad or constrained. Was data and decision-making transparent across teams or was it limited to within silos (and, as per Andrew Blain, were those silos expanding into chasms)? Did that transparency extend to metrics, especially metrics regarding how teams worked to deliver targets and maintain flow?

When we commenced our work with InsureCo, we took a similar approach. The fundamentals were a bit different, of course. Their focus on providing insurance meant that being people-first, and helping people live better lives, was already a core driver of this organization. In fact, annual engagement surveys demonstrated that employees did feel supported by their organization.

Did this extend to how InsureCo structured control of the work in delivery teams? Unfortunately, not. It was by no means universal, but in some domains, (even the more progressive ones) we discovered prescriptive governance that treated people like cogs in a larger machine. Engagement was low, with teams feeling disempowered and being viewed as feature factories. This was the result of an intentional divide being opened between demand and supply, between those who wanted the change and those who were actually able to make the change. The final impact was overburdening, a lack of clarity, and challenges to alignment in strategic outcomes, which had all evolved as a result of long-term decisions, management policies, and interventions.

To shift this system, we asked management to take a human-first approach to redesigning their operating model. We provided each team domain with tools that would help them design their ideal working and governance models, and stayed hands-on to guide them through the process. This approach leveraged the Remote:af model as well as the principles within the five stanchions, while being contextualized to the existing systems within InsureCo.

We needed to ensure that any work done to change and evolve governance models was done with an awareness of existing constraints that could inhibit change, and to standardize data so that each team could clearly understand how the system traced work from strategy to done.

All of this required trust—not always easy to come by, we know! When in doubt, we returned to Principle Five of the Manifesto: *"Build projects around motivated individuals. Give them the environment and support they need, and trust them to get the job done."*

We also asked, do we provide the space to collaboratively design their work? Principle 8 states: *"Agile processes promote sustainable development. The sponsors, developers, and users should be able to maintain a constant pace indefinitely."*

Those two principles were our guiding light with InsureCo. We supplied guidance and the pattern to follow and then carved out the time to enable teams to learn and design together. The people on the ground did the rest.

But our time with InsureCo raised a question we just couldn't shake: why, exactly, do so many systems of governance seem to want to minimize or strip away the humanity from their teams? We see Prudential Standards, Prudential Guidelines, and Reporting Standards… and almost none of it is human-centric! In fact, much of the Governance ecosystem eschews the carrot and instead uses the regulatory or compliance stick based on those standards to expedite or block work. This, in turn, creates unnecessary tension.

Our experience spent using Humanity as the Cornerstone and a driver for crafting Agile Governance has allowed us to turn this on its head, even in heavily regulated industries. We'd often hear (in response to our proposals), "Your ideas can't work here because we are heavily regulated." In these instances, we responded with, "Regulated more than a nuclear submarine?" We'd then provide the context of Turn the Ship Around[80], where David Marquet used principles similar to our stanchions to turn the Santa Fe Nuclear Submarine from the worst to the best performing in the Navy. In these High Reliability categorized organizations (HRO[81]), interactive complexity and tight coupling can, theoretically, lead to a system accident—a failure more critical than a simple loss of productivity, for example. Marquet achieved this through strong organizational design, a culture focused on safety, clear management, and the most critical factor of all: empowering the right people to make decisions. If he could turn decades, if not centuries of traditional governance on its head in a HRO without breaking regulations, why can't others?

When we talk about people making choices and decisions, and a culture of governance that helps accelerate decision-making, there's no example that matches the Santa Fe Nuclear Submarine. We want to be clear that transitioning to a human-centric system of governance doesn't change the fundamental goals of that system: the intent and the outcome. All we want to do is accelerate the pace of critical decision-making. The reason for setting practices and methods to control and report on work is also unchanged. What we believe and work towards is changing the *how* and the *what*, and even then, we're not asking for a complete reinvention.

This is in contrast to when a new leader arrives, recognizes problems in how the current system is working, and (in the pursuit of increased efficiency and effectiveness) chooses the most disruptive option. Go nuclear! Blow everything up and let the pieces land where they may! This approach refuses to acknowledge the current state of the existing system and presupposes that

---

[80] L David Marquet (2012). Turn the ship around!: how to create leadership at every level. Austin, Tex.: Greenleaf Book Group Press.
[81] Dave van Stralen, Tom Mercer, Karl Weick, Karlene Roberts. (n.d.). https://www.high-reliability.org/

everything is wrong and irredeemable. In some scenarios, this may be correct. In many (most) others, work needs to commence with a more human-centric approach. Before change commences, the existing system needs to be analyzed so both good and bad can be identified. That means picking out the constraints, the things that work and should be retained, and what aspects can be leveraged for broader benefit and to accelerate change. This approach also builds better human engagement, as it places the people within the system at the heart of the change process.

In a complex environment, when responding to VUCA, we often don't know in advance what the truly impactful activities are going to be. So, instead of blowing everything up, preserve as many options as possible to the last responsible moment[82].

Another option is greenfields—creating an all-new structure or system alongside the existing system that can eventually be attached or subsumed into the original. Or strangle the old, to borrow the "Strangler Pattern" metaphor from Martin Fowler[83]: *"...gradually create a new system around the edges of the old, letting it grow slowly over several years until the old system is strangled."*

However, building a new structure or system without awareness and connectivity to the existing system creates more problems than it solves. Setting up a tribe, putting in your own train lines, or whatever your flavor of change vehicle, is often done in ignorance of the broader system and how real change happens. As a result, the Law of Unintended Consequences[84] (outcomes of a

---

[82] To learn more about the last responsible moment, we recommend Poppendieck, M. and Poppendieck, T. (2003). Lean Software Development: An Agile Toolkit. Sydney: Pearson Education, Limited.

[83] Fowler, M. (2019). The Strangler Fig Application. Available at: https://martinfowler.com/bliki/StranglerFigApplication.html.

[84] Law of unintended consequences. (n.d.). https://www.sas.upenn.edu/~haroldfs/540/handouts/french/unintconseq.html

purposeful action that are not intended or foreseen), comes into play, although there's enough evidence to demonstrate those outcomes are entirely predictable and are repeated every time. Unintended, yes. Unpredictable? No.

What's critical to us is the essence of agility itself, about putting people first. The Agile Manifesto was a moment in time designed to challenge systems of work that hampered pro-knowledge work and pro-creative environments. We must now expand upon the manifesto and find ways to include people in our larger governance decisions. And not just the people *within* the newly transformed ecosystem, but those in and around the system required to get work done and value shipped.

We observed the necessity of Humanity as the Cornerstone when working with InsureCo. We quickly learned how important the psychosocial element of transformation was. When people have been asked to operate in a certain way for so long, and learned not to challenge the status quo, it takes a long time for them to feel empowered enough to fully embrace the opportunity of change. Even their leaders tended to defer to the current working model, refusing to see the value of allowing humans to design how they want to work. Nothing to see here, they insisted. Just copy the existing approach.

We also saw a tendency amongst leaders where, post design decisions, they would re-prosecute and push back against those decisions. The result was that they lacked the trust of their teams. Of course, that's okay if emergent data and information not previously known casts new light on previous decisions. It's often leaders who receive the greatest breadth of information flow, as opposed to people lower in the hierarchical system. But as far as we observed, that often wasn't the driver behind this behavior.

Towards the end of our engagement with InsureCo, we found that feedback from the teams taking part in the new design approach was as mixed as the feedback from leaders. Some had dived into the challenge of creating change and wanted to own the process. Some viewed it as getting in the way of work. People are nonlinear and unpredictable. However, that unpredictability can also be a strength, if leveraged correctly.

As a public service entity rather than a private-sector organization, GovCo already had a higher focus on people than the norm. However, in much the same way as we've observed in the private sector, this often translated to the leadership group but not all the way through to the people doing the work.

In this case, the people working on the program had become engaged, empowered, and passionate about their way of working. Yet this was counterbalanced by frustration as the governing mechanisms of the organization were at loggerheads with what they knew was working well, and they didn't have the capacity to solve this mismatch.

The change program had enabled teams to be self-organizing, granting individuals autonomy and ownership. It acknowledged their intelligence and creativity, which fostered trust, respect, and empowerment. By encouraging open communication and collaboration, they had created a sense of belonging and shared purpose among team members. The vital aspect of continuous learning and improvement was embraced and celebrated, along with frequent feedback loops, enabling individuals to learn, adapt, and enhance their skills. However, a continued focus on the traditional mechanistic processes of the organization, rather than an understanding of the humanistic attributes of agility, was eroding the benefits gained.

We were able to make this conflict visible to teams and leaders alike by using the focus of the Humanity stanchion. We demonstrated to the relevant parties how the ways in which they were working did or didn't align with what the organization had come to expect. This process took time. And was still a work in progress when we last engaged with them. However, what we saw at that time, was leadership beginning to embrace the new way of working, and understanding the humanistic focus, which was already creating results that mechanistic processes could not achieve.

Until now, we haven't discussed our work with Remote:af as it pertains to the stanchion of Humanity as the Cornerstone. Why? Because, when we applied our ideas about governance to develop the remote governance functionality for the Remote Agility Framework, we didn't specifically name Humanity as a pillar.

This was because the framework already had a deep commitment to including humanity as one of its fundamental purposes for existence. We didn't need to inject more humanity into the framework. We merely ensured that elements of remote governance wrapped themselves around those concepts to ensure that they considered human interactions.

The founder of Remote:af, Andrew Blain, anticipated that COVID-19 would cause widespread societal shutdowns and businesses would need to transition to remote working in order to survive. This gave the impetus to design a remote-first way of working that could mimic human interactions, but moving to digital first and indeed governing the entire system of work was paramount to enabling this.

Remote:af's remote governance, of course, made use of agile and had a sharp focus on enabling the framework to handle human conditions generated by the sudden (and, as we now know, new normal) shift to remote working. Those conditions were the loss of visibility, control, connection, and learned helplessness.

In order to begin incorporating the Humanity stanchion into your own organization, we recommend you:

1. **Familiarize yourself with the Heart of Agile:** Learn about Dr. Alistair Cockburn's model for simplifying and clarifying the critical imperatives of agility. Understand the emphasis on people and human interactions as the cornerstone of good governance.

2. **Reflect on the importance of humanity in governance:** Consider how your current governance practices prioritize and incorporate the human element. Assess whether your organization's culture promotes psychological safety, trust, transparency, and collaboration among teams.

3. **Adopt a human-centric approach to governance:** If your governance practices seem to minimize or strip away humanity from teams, explore ways to shift towards a more human-centric system. Embrace principles like empowerment, trust, and a culture focused on safety.

4. **Analyze and improve your existing system:** Before making disruptive changes, take the time to analyze your current governance system. Identify the constraints and the aspects that are working well and can be leveraged for broader benefits. Use this information to build better human engagement in the change process.

5. **Explore remote governance:** If your organization has moved to remote or asynchronous work, consider exploring remote governance frameworks like Remote:af. Focus on incorporating human interactions and addressing the challenges associated with remote work, such as loss of visibility, control, connection, and learned helplessness.

By taking these actions, you can begin to understand and implement the importance of humanity as the cornerstone of good governance, leading to more effective and human-centric approaches to decision-making and work management.

13

Don't Stand Still

Through our time spent developing the Agile Governance model and the five stanchions, a common question we ask ourselves is: what's the final purpose of this work? What is agility's endgame, and the endgame of Agile Governance?

The answer lies in the original Agile Manifesto. For example, we look to principle #10: *"Simplicity—the art of maximizing the amount of work not done—is essential."*

Good governance should create an environment where people are productive, engaged, and feel a sense of ownership, while also protecting those people, their shareholders, and external stakeholders from harm. It should strip away the non-essentials so that driven professionals can spend their time on what truly matters. These theories are not new—in fact, they have been at the heart of Lean thinking since the formulation of the Toyota Production System. Bad governance is a collection of competing principles and regulations that function as effectively as a bag of snakes. Good, Agile Governance should be simple and understandable. In fact, the more we simplify over time, the better our governance becomes. There is always the risk of oversimplification, and although we seek to remove waste, we must be wary of simplifying so much that we create untenable risk. There is always a balance required.

We're also big fans of principle #9: *"Continuous attention to technical excellence and good design enhances agility."*

Most organizations are used to pursuing technical excellence and good design in their development teams. At least they say they are, and it comes as a sticker on the package when you buy the goods. We want to normalize pursuing technical excellence and good design in our governance. The tools we use to measure and analyze, to communicate and enable, or the design of systems and spaces that build transparency and collaboration, are all an end-goal of good governance. So, take that principle and apply it more broadly.

There is one principle that underpins and elevates all others. Not the icing on the cake, but the flour that binds the cake together. Specifically, the final principle: *"At regular intervals, the team reflects on how to become more effective, then tunes and adjusts its behavior accordingly."*

This concluding principle, in our opinion, is key to the entire purpose and mindset of agility: constant and continuous evolution. This is echoed in the opening line of the manifesto: *"We are uncovering better ways of developing software."*

We *are uncovering*. Not *we have uncovered*. To be agile is to always be exploring, discovering, and improving. This, we feel, is the true endgame of agility. Terminology, processes, and tools… can and will change shape over time. But the core of the matter—to continuously reflect, learn, grow, and evolve—is pivotal.

It also starts with *we*, not *us* or *you*. This is critical, and when we think about good governance, it always has an element of distributed governance. Everybody within the system must play a part in ensuring that the principles, practices, and processes put in place are able to be executed by the people. This builds trust. Risk is a good example of this: most organizations will have the concept of first, second, and third-line risks, each managed by a different set of employees. The first line (or, in military parlance, the front line) are people specifically named as risk managers. They have a key role and responsibility, and they know it. By the time you get down to the third line, you're often referring to people for whom managing risk is a part of their responsibility but not specifically defined as their role. These are the people you often need to empower within your organization to deliver customer outcomes. As such, the risk they manage is no less important. Risk must be approached as an *"us"* issue, or trust won't be an *"us"* concept.

Continuous evolution is more than a recipe for improvement. It's also a survival principle. Long before agility was a common term in business theory, the same principles were being applied by industry greats. Toyota manufactured textile looms before they broke into the automotive industry. Kiichiro Toyoda, son of Toyoda Loom Works founder Sakichi Toyoda, was an innovative engineer who experimented with and embraced steam, oil, and electric looms. When their factory was robbed and their groundbreaking designs stolen, Kiichiro said: *"The thieves may be able to follow the design plans and produce a loom. But we are modifying and improving our looms every day. They do not have the expertise gained from the failures it took to produce the original. We need not be concerned. We need only continue as always, making our improvements."*[85]

In 1937, Kiichiro Toyoda would take the family business in new directions with the founding of Toyota Motor Corporation. A continuous evolution mindset propelled a small but successful loom manufacturer into the annals of history.

This is where we hope the five stanchions of Agile Governance can take you, as well.

This principle of continuous evolution is expressed in the term we chose to describe the five essential cores of Agile Governance: stanchion. A stanchion is not a concrete pillar or a piece of foundation. It's a sturdy, upright fixture that supports other objects

---

[85] Kiichiro Toyoda, quoted in 2008, 'Toyota Quotes', *New York Times*, 10 Feb

until they can become fixed in place. Could you use a stanchion as a permanent fixture? Sure, if necessary. We'd love to see the stanchions as strong enough to always support you and your organization in reaching your shared objectives. But, ultimately, the shape of the stanchions suits the need. You don't build a house to fit the shape of pre-existing scaffolding; you put up the scaffolding to suit the home.

In fact, our understanding of the stanchions is continuously evolving as well. Yes, we've put them into practice at multiple organizations—and to great effect. We've also had the opportunity to reshape them in different contexts, like our time at Remote:af. All of these experiences served to show us just how much we don't yet know, and how much room the stanchions have to grow.

We're not the only ones who can grow the five stanchions. You can too. How you adapt them, incorporate them, and customize them to suit your goals and the goals of your organization, is what brings them to life. The variability of how you apply the stanchions is what allows them to be properly harnessed to create value and opportunity. In fact, that variability is the heart of the stanchions, and of agility. The freedom to adapt, learn, and grow the ways in which you apply the stanchions is what will give your governance longevity and strength.

That's why we propose you think of the stanchions not as a strict model to be followed, but as a collection of questions and principles that prompt you to inspect and adapt your own Agile Governance frame of reference to suit the needs of your business and the needs of your customers. We want you questioning, examining, probing, experimenting, and reflecting in a way that makes the stanchions your own... and most importantly of all, *continuously evolving.* It would be thrilling to see readers with their own, bespoke adaptations of the five stanchions that suit their own forms of governance and the needs of their customers.

When we discuss variability, we like to paraphrase Dave Snowden. He once said that you should never have perfect transparency because it eliminates variability. It becomes a "solved game", to borrow a phrase from our friends in the competitive Checkers and Go communities[86]. A little bit of opacity forces people to think outside the box and create new solutions. In other words, variability is where your competitive advantage lies. In fact, over-application of strict methods and processes in a creative domain will limit your ability to exploit variability for your benefit. When we think about designing patterns and ways of working, they need to vary by domain for this very reason. Different problems have different solutions.

You need to harness this power. The stanchions—or whichever model you choose to help build effective Governance—provide anchors to align around. You, as an individual and an organization, need to find the points of variability—the skills, knowledge, and approaches that make your work singular and powerful—and use them to carve out a space in the modern economy.

This discussion of variability and adaptation raises an important question: how far can you move away from the stanchions before they stop functioning as intended?

Excellent question. There are degrees of freedom in how you interpret and apply the learnings behind the five stanchions, and they were designed to be flexible for both adaptation and learning. The initial concepts behind the stanchions function well as anchors; however, as soon as you step outside the book and begin applying

---

[86] Checkers, AKA Draughts, has been "weak-solved", meaning that players who know how to play perfectly can always at least force a draw. Go, on the other hand, is a much larger game. It has been weak-solved if played on a miniature board (7x7 squares), but there are more potential moves on a 19x19 Go board than there are atoms in the universe, so that solve might be a little way off. For more information, check https://en.wikipedia.org/wiki/Solved_game

this knowledge to your own organization, you're going to discover a lot of places where our learnings and yours won't fit together perfectly.

That's because, while the five stanchions of Agile Governance are a frame of reference to help support your own governance, they're more in the style of Clayton Christensen[87]. That is, a framework without a framework.

What does that mean?

Consider martial arts. When you learn martial arts, one of the first and most important lessons to internalize is that the *volume* of what you know is less important than the *quality*. A thousand poorly executed techniques will not serve you as well as one or two executed with speed, accuracy, and control. To understand how to perform a technique with quality, you need to steep yourself in the foundations of that martial art: the footwork, patterns, weight transfer, body control, and so on.

The more you learn about those fundamentals, the more you realize how much there is to learn. We know this through our own experiences as martial artists. Earning a black belt in karate wasn't an endpoint, it was a moment when we reflected and realized we'd only just gotten a grip on the basics. Now, the real learning could begin. Sensei Lucky Pandelidis from the Winged Dragon Go Ju Ryu dojo, who we were fortunate enough to train with, always says he can't wait for people to qualify for Shodan-ho[88], the first black belt. Only then can he start to actually teach them karate.

We've also seen what happens when people move away from those fundamentals. Oftentimes, it's not good. That's how you get flashy techniques with no practical application. When you see people in the ring sparring without those fundamentals, you notice

---

[87] Christensen, C.M., Efosa Ojomo and Dillon, K. (2019). The prosperity paradox: How innovation can lift nations out of poverty. New York, Ny: Harper Business.
[88] https://en.wikipedia.org/wiki/Shodan_(rank)

gaps in their patterns. They lack sustainability and, ironically, the flexibility provided by drilling the fundamentals. Interestingly, these people can be dangerous because they're unpredictable and lack control. In the ring so as in business: take extra caution when encountering someone with the power to make an impact and no idea how to wield it.

It's the same in governance. Every governance structure will be unique, but if you abandon the foundations then you'll end up back where you started: flashy technique piled atop flashy technique until you end up with a massive organizational construct teetering under its own weight. Humans tend to overcomplicate, which leads us to reflect on Gall's Law. *"A complex system that works is invariably found to have evolved from a simple system that worked. A complex system designed from scratch never works and cannot be patched up to make it work. You have to start over with a working simple system."*[89]

Many organizations that we work with today and consider progressive, sustainable, and keeping ahead of their competition, have taken the view that ongoing transformation is critical to their success. Transformation is becoming a capability rather than a state in and of itself. In one organization we are actively trying to discourage the use of the word *transformation* because of the implications that there is an end state—to be transformed—which will then lead to inertia later on. We are trying to nudge the static culture of that organization closer to a place of constant evolution of their practices and processes. In another organization, we've done a lot of work to reclaim and recontextualize the word *transformation*, so that it is something known within that organization's culture as an ongoing activity. The reasons are simple. If you are not changing, adapting, and moving forward

[89] Gall, J. (1979). *Systematics: how systems work and especially how they fail.* London: Fontana.

compared to the pace of change and complexity around you, you are essentially going backwards. Your competition is not standing still. And neither are the people who want to be your competitor.

It takes a certain organizational mindset to slow down and work on mastering the basics before moving on to unique implementations. A rare mindset, you might say. We've seen a lot of instances where an organization detects a problem and then creates a new process or control to manage it. Problem solved, right? Time to move on.

The problem here is that nobody is slowing down to assess whether that control or process aligns with the framework. They're not asking, "what did we learn while solving this problem?" The urge is always to move onward as fast as possible instead of returning to the basics, comparing with the new ways, and growing as a result.

So, how can you begin a process of continuous evolution that actively moves your governance forward without falling into the trap of creating unnecessary controls? How, as you move forward with applying the five stanchions to your own governance, can you stay aware of what your organization needs and be ready to continually inspect and adapt your own Agile Governance?

You can't start from a static position. You have to get out there and start by wading into the weeds. Begin by moving towards the new and experimental practices we've discussed in the stanchions... and those in the coming chapters. You can't wait for solutions to present themselves. The only way to succeed is to uncover them yourselves.

That said, we do have a few recommended techniques for you to explore as a foundation for building great Agile Governance.

14
Enabling Governance

In Chapter 13, we explored the final, most critical agile principle: *"At regular intervals, the team reflects on how to become more effective, then tunes and adjusts its behavior accordingly."*

This, in our opinion, is key to the entire purpose and mindset of agility: constant and continuous evolution. This is echoed in the opening line of the manifesto: *"We are uncovering better ways of developing software."*

With the operative word being *uncovering*. To truly be an agile organization, learning and adaptation must never stop. The world is VUCA, change is constant, so governance should always be evolving.

While the stanchions themselves are permanent fixtures, how you organize around them to bring your own governance structure to life is where variability emerges. In variability, we find opportunity.

In this book, we've provided the overarching principles. We've explored questions you can ask to interrogate the existing system and, we hope, build a better one atop the bones of the old. However, the actual learning and growth must be done by you, in your own context.

Enabling Agile Governance in the Real World

At this point in the conversation—with you, the reader, immersed in the theory of Agile Governance and how the five stanchions can provide new lenses through which to examine your organization— it's tempting to begin recommending specific techniques or processes that can move your organization towards a culture and mindset of continuous improvement.

We could list a million of them here, if we wanted. They'd all be useful in one way or another. However, would they suit your organizational context and help you become more dynamic and adaptive, or would they end up tying you down to traditional governance methods?

Our mission with Agile Governance (and with this book) has been to move people away from traditional methods and governing mechanisms that constrain their ability to become a dynamically adaptive organization. We want your organization to be ready to adapt at pace, to make changes throughout that are driven by the people closest to the work. We want to enable you to adopt decentralized, autonomous decisioning underpinned by the five stanchions. All of this is critical in a world of increasing complexity and volatility, where the business landscape is changing faster than we can track.

That sort of decisioning won't happen if a central collective of decision-makers are prescribing a set of rigid techniques.

Yet, this is what we see all the time. Organizations know they need to be more reactive to deal with a VUCA landscape, so leadership insists their teams adopt methods X, Y, and Z regardless of whether they're appropriate for the team or customer. This is reactive demand management, often based on long-cycle planning. Short-term changes appear agile, but if they're still in service to a larger plan they may not be appropriate for the organization's needs, or account for the internal VUCA. They look outward without reflecting inward.

This sort of traditional governance is slow, bureaucratic, and usually based upon heavyweight business cases focused on cost. Dynamically Adaptive Organizations[90], on the other hand, base their decisions on continuous value flow. Their governance is fundamentally agile and distributed, so they're able to adapt in relevant ways and at the right speed to solve problems before those problems change. They can experiment and innovate in tighter cycles, enabling continuous improvement. They're also aware of internal VUCA because they take the time to reflect. Their changes are made to suit both external and internal demands and they can choose and experiment with the processes and techniques that best suit those specific needs.

We can't provide you with a checklist on how to make those changes, nor should you expect leadership to either. Instead, make sure decision-making is distributed to the people doing the work so they can uncover and implement what best suits them and their organization's needs.

What we can do is give you some methods we have used and observed being used successfully, methods that might be applicable to your particular context.

We have split these ideas into two core elements: the Heart; and the Hands. Both are needed and have differing perspectives. It's a little socio-technical, a little mechanistic, a little humanistic, and a lot of being and doing.

The Heart is about inspiring people, about the culture of the organization, and about how you need to work with people to guide how they see, feel, behave, and act towards the future. Embodying the why and taking people on a journey

The Hands are the processes, methods, and practices; they're

---

[90] Ponton, T. (2023) https://www.remoteaf.co/insights

the actions that are taken to move towards the goal. The ways of working and tooling that enable better governance—the practical application you can see and do. Let's start with the Hands.

14.1 The Hands that Act

Go With the Flow

You already know that we consider data crucial to effective governance. We wouldn't have built an entire stanchion around it if we thought otherwise. So, if you're aiming to create a cycle of continuous improvement, your goal must be to find new ways of applying data to the governance itself. This should serve to elevate information around the governance's performance and highlight where that governance is improving.

Use your own data. Gather it, analyze it, and use it to drive change. Measure that change and reflect upon it to continually optimize your systems of governance. Using Flow based principles is a great way to do this as when adopted holistically it comes with an amazing set of powerful data and insights that can be drawn from it.

Which is easy to say. Maybe more complicated to put into practice. What we've observed is that many leaders and organizations *say* that they're data-driven. They insist that they make data-driven decisions all the time. But once you dig deeper, you find major decisions being made on gut feeling. Until you break out of that mindset, it doesn't matter what you measure or how you analyze it. Your system of governance will never truly be optimized, and your data will be wasted.

If you're serious about being data-driven, then don't just pay lip-service. Commit to it. Turn the lens onto yourself and be ruthless when it comes to weeding out opinion-led decisions. If you find yourself reverting to opinion or gut feeling, stop. Ask, do we have enough data to make this decision? If not, is that why we're reverting to our old ways? What do we need to measure? How can we measure it? Refuse to move forward until you have the facts in hand.

Retrospect

Retrospectives are a well-trodden and well-understood technique in agile, and are a foundational principle of continuously reflecting, learning, and evolving. In fact, we've been fortunate enough to meet the people who wrote the book on retrospectives: Diana Larsen, Esther Derby, and Ken Schwaber. We'd call their book *Agile Retrospectives: Making Good Teams Great* [91] an essential read, especially if you feel your retrospectives aren't helping to achieve measurable change.

A good retrospective is about learning and understanding. We've seen a lot of fantastic retros in our time. We've also seen organizations where retros don't seem to lead to any positive change. We call these sorts of processes and rituals "Forrest Gumps", because we see people running, running, running endlessly. You ask, where are you running to? They don't know. Why are you running at all? They don't know. When are you going to stop? They don't know that either.

This is a symptom we see in organizations where there's a colossal amount of pressure to achieve newer, shinier, bigger things. Retrospectives are performed, yet nobody has the opportunity to reflect upon or apply the learnings. Traditionally it would be the Project Implementation Review (PIR). Usually at the end, post closure of a fixed planned initiative, to gather lessons learned—which sit in a file somewhere that no one knows about, knows they need, or can even find.

If you want to improve your governance and systems of work,

---

[91] Esther Derby (Author), Diana Larsen (Author), Ken Schwaber (Author, Foreword)

you need to take the time in your retrospectives to breathe and ask, what's working for us? What isn't? What can we improve, and how can we achieve it?

Otherwise, you'll end up with a lot of forward motion that gets you nowhere, like chasing a mirage. You need to adopt a Kaizen-style mentality that embraces continuous improvement rather than using retrospectives as a checked box, and you can't improve if you don't know what needs improving.

Interestingly, running in the same place for too long is doubly dangerous because it gives you the illusion of stability. You might assume everything is okay because at least you're still performing at the same level you were twelve or eighteen months ago. In reality, everyone else has raced ahead. Relative to your competitors, and your customers' needs, you've fallen well behind. In this, business matches one of the fundamental laws of thermodynamics: [92]energy will naturally bleed from a higher to a lower temperature object, but never in the other direction. If you want to stay hot, and on the bleeding edge, you need to inject fresh energy into the system.

So, don't be a Forrest Gump. Know where you're headed, why you're going there, and how you're going to improve, and do this all via retrospectives.

Kaizen

In case you missed it in earlier chapters: Kaizen is a Japanese term that means change for the better. In agile terms, Continuous Improvement.

Some people use Kaizen as if it's a process or tool. We'd rather think of it as a mindset and goal. We love the stanchions because they ask you to reflect upon your systems of governance in a way

---

[92] First Law of Thermodynamics. (n.d.). https://www.grc.nasa.gov/www/k-12/airplane/thermo1.html

that trends towards continuous improvement. In other words, Kaizen is baked into the stanchions from the ground up.

Kaizen stands at the polar opposite of Kaikaku; also Japanese and meaning radical change. Big Bang changes that are radical in scope, speed, and level of disruption have their time and place, but they're not what the Kaizen philosophy is all about. We'd rather ask, what's the next problem we can identify? How can I plan for it, begin the process with potential solutions, check the efficacy of those solutions, and then act upon what I know? (AKA, the Deming cycle). How can I create a mindset and vision for continuous evolution that keeps not just myself or my team, but the entire organization, working through that cycle?

We've worked with a number of organizations that wanted to nurture this sort of thinking. They tried, once or twice. However, since it didn't work the first time, it didn't stick. What did we do wrong, they asked?

The answer is most often, "You stopped."

These organizations wanted continuous evolution minus the iterative process. They want to cut out the messy parts: the failures, learning, growth, changes in shape, improvements, more failures, more learning, and so on. They want the copy and paste formula applied to organizations, often found in a glossy 400 slide PowerPoint presentation provided to solve your problems.

We see this in other areas, too. In leadership, or in the restructuring of systems of governance. A once-off effort that achieves part of what it set out to do and is then left to stagnate.

That's not Kaizen, and it's certainly not effective. Our five stanchions, on the other hand, are all about making informed, incremental changes. And then, as soon as one change is acted upon, moving on to the next. And the next. And the next.

We understand that, when it comes to governance, a lot of continuous evolution is constrained by regulation. Various regulatory bodies will arrive and ask for you to show them your controls, your processes. To do this, you must define those processes. And with every process that's rigidly defined, you lose a fraction of flexibility.

We've already shared our feelings on whether regulators are the great enemy of improvement (they aren't); however, they do require us to think in different ways about what regulations are and how governance functions. Regulation can either guide us towards new solutions or crush creativity and innovation.

You want to enable the former.

So, to create a Kaizen mindset and environment, you need to make sure your teams have the skills and knowledge required to operate in an agile way inside the guide rails of regulation. That means uplifting your risk assessment frameworks and control frameworks in an ongoing manner to improve upon them, and as you learn new information. Risk assessments and control frameworks are important tools when thinking about how to govern a system, and while we won't explore them in-depth in this book, we strongly recommend you integrate them into your patterns of work.

Heart of Agile

Dr. Alistair Cockburn, one of the authors of the *Agile Software Development Manifesto*, developed The Heart of Agile (HOA), which is a fantastic tool for considering how you can improve and adapt. Using the HOA's four guiding principles—Collaborate, Deliver, Reflect, and Improve—you can examine your organizational constructs against the Stanchions to start making changes and then use them to continually evolve and change in a considered manner.

We'll briefly explore these four principles.

Collaborate: In order to grow trust and motivation, and accelerate the flow of information, collaboration needs to be improved. To do this, we look to improve the collaborative connective tissues that allow information to flow horizontally, vertically, and bi-directionally. This in turn creates a culture of transparency and, ultimately, trust. This enables you to implement Agile Governance, its directional decisions, and elevates your ability to deliver outcomes.

Deliver: The ability to make expedient and informed directional decisions means that in governing your system of work you can focus not only on delivering incrementally, early, and often for early value, but also enables you to deliver and create learnings for continuous improvement.

Reflect and Improve: Provide an essential way to examine your Collaboration and Delivery based on the data and information generated from delivery. Reflecting and improving are inextricably entwined and often thought of as the same act. However, many organizations simply jump to improving without stopping to examine and understand the context. Therefore, the Heart of Agile separates them to ensure focus.

Reflect: Data is examined, whether subjective or objective, through data analysis. Reflection is used because it can be a combination of retrospection, known and used so well in agile, and introspection. Actual insights are generated to fuel improvement.

Improve: Based on those insights, rapid learning (probe, sense, and respond) is used to understand and create effective actions. Those actions are then used to adapt the governing of your systems of work.

Remote:af®: Remote Governance System

As we wrote earlier, we used the concepts of the Stanchions to create the "Pillars of Remote Governance" for **Remote:af**.

The Remote:af team have worked with Esther Derby to co-create a "remote governance system". This system provides leaders and organizations with a way to understand and identify meaningful ways to evolve and enable the way they govern their organizations.

The "remote governance system"© is made up of a set of modules that leverage patterns, tools, and exercises that have been developed using the Esther Derby SEEM© model and Remote:af governance patterns.

The system uses a set of principles, structures, and patterns that enable leaders to navigate the governance system and explore unknowns in order to:

- understand and identify meaningful ways to evolve the system of governance as a whole within your own context;
- increase the zone of transparency in a rational way;
- purposefully adjust leadership for remote spaces;
- create the collaborative linkages that enable information flow;
- leverage data for dynamic analysis and decision-making;
- establish the basis for trust in remote/hybrid spaces.

If you're feeling stuck at the beginning of your Agile Governance journey, we highly recommend taking a look at the Remote:af system and how it can support you. Start your exploration at https://www.remoteaf.co/tool/improve-evolve-enable-remote-governance

Now we move on to the Heart.

14.2 The Heart that Guides

Empowerment

To create a culture of continuous improvement, you need everyone in an organization to have a certain degree of power. They need the capacity to reflect upon their work, processes, and relationships with governance, as well as the ability to make changes where necessary that better serve customers and colleagues.

The problem is that traditional governance concentrates decision-making authority in a few select individuals, and then places those individuals at the head of a top-down structure. It is, by definition, disempowering.

The alternative approach is to create distributed, participatory governance. This does more than put decision-making in the hands of more people. It turns those people into a broad range of stakeholders. It empowers a greater selection of people to get more granular in their planning and execution and increases their investment in the process and outcomes.

So, how can we empower people to make these decisions and become more invested in outcomes?

The answers lie, as before, in the stanchions. We start with information flow: both horizontally and vertically through the connective tissues of the organization. Without that flow, people can't make decisions. Restrict that flow, and you disempower them. We also see that disempowered people are less likely to share information in the first place. This creates further risk by strangling the flow of data. Traditional project milestones, quarterly reporting approaches, steering committees, and so on take information sharing away from teams and concentrate it in the hands of leadership. The result: by the time leadership realizes something is wrong, it's too late to change and adapt.

Empower your people. Give them a reason to invest in customer outcomes. Allow them to communicate in the ways that they need. All of this will enable greater agility in your governance and create the environment necessary for continuous improvement.

Customer Centricity

Customer expectations are already continuously improving, or at least, continuously evolving as improvement is in the eye of the beholder. However, the rise of customer expectations and demands has not always been in lockstep with organizations realizing their need to be more customer-centric. We've already talked about how companies must ensure their decision-making processes are customer-centric, lest they fall behind or collapse entirely. That's why our entire approach to the five stanchions is customer-driven, and we recommend aligning your governance to customer needs if you want to always be growing and improving.

Some organizations struggle with this paradigm shift. They're stuck in a pre-Copernican mindset of still believing that the customer revolves around the business. They expect the customer to come to them, bowing and scraping, as opposed to bringing their services to the customer. When you tell them to adjust their worldview, they get angry. Remember that Copernicus was reviled during his lifetime by Protestant protestors, who refused the notion that the earth revolved around the sun… and sixty years after his death, the Catholic Church took action against his publications. Yet, Copernican theory is now a fundamental tenet of astronomy.

In the same fashion, organizations that refuse to recognize the necessity of customer centricity are wasting their breath and losing customer share. Only by examining how you engage with your customers and meet their needs can you gain the competitive edge needed.

So, if you want to make strides towards Agile Governance, start with your customers. What aspects of your governance serve them, and which serve yourself? Which advances in technology and information sharing help your customers to make informed choices, and which keep them in the dark?

If in doubt, choose the customer. If you can't meet their needs, reflect upon your governance processes and experiment until you can. That's the true impetus behind continuous improvement.

Technology and the Art of Living Digitally

All of the new ways of working and governing explored in this book are only possible because of radical advances in technology. Many software platforms and solutions we now consider standard parts of the office suite have only seen widespread adoption since 2020, and it's that technology that has allowed us to effectively gather and leverage data and insights. In short, our technology platforms are already continuously evolving, for better or worse. It's up to us to keep pace.

That's why our approach with the stanchions embraces technology-driven governance that allows us to make informed decisions more effectively. The faster and more informed our decisions, the better we're able to break out of the loop of extended, centralized decisioning cycles. We must break out of those cycles if we want to create effective governance.

The problem is that many organizations don't realize they're trapped in these cycles. They adopt traditional processes—often driven by traditional technology—that pile up and pile up until they form a tower of rubbish functioning less as governance and more as a form of organizational duress.

To continue with the tower of rubbish analogy, do you know what happens when garbage decomposes? It generates methane. Poison. No wonder organizations struggling beneath the weight of traditional systems and technology struggle to retain their best talent. How can culture flourish when everyone is breathing poison? How can you blame talent for leaving when they see other organizations adopting new technologies that replace the rubbish and cleans the air?

Traditional governance simply doesn't align with the expectations and preferences of the modern workforce, or the technology they use on a day-to-day basis. Employees value autonomy, transparency, and purpose. This is a generational shift that's quantifiable through data.

Technology is in a state of continuous evolution, whether you adopt it or not. The needs and expectations of potential talent are evolving to match. You'll need continuous evolution within your own organization if you don't want to fall behind.

Cultural Evolution or Revolution?

We just mentioned generational changes in how new talent perceives their work, goals, technology, and the relationships they require with leadership and governance.

This is the essence of the fifth stanchion, Humanity as the Cornerstone. To place people at the heart of your governance and decision-making is to acknowledge that people are always in a state of continuous evolution. The needs of your customers, teams, and stakeholders, are always growing and changing. Organizations that embrace this and, in turn, embrace alternate governance methods such as what can be achieved via the five stanchions, can create a more inclusive and empowering culture that attracts the best talent of the day.

This is the reality of culture. An organization can try to create a culture—by allowing or disallowing certain behaviors and mindsets—but it will also form dynamically based upon the methods and processes you use, the standards you embody, and the

218

ways in which you govern. When you use traditional methods of command and control, you're unlikely to foster a modern, inclusive culture that can self-direct and self-govern.

Traditional governance may also deny these evolutions in culture and the support they need to thrive. The first fish to flap their way out of the sea almost 400 million years ago probably would've appreciated a hand off the beach. They would've resented leadership gently nudging them back into the surf because deadlines were too pressing to experiment with breathing on land.

This is why we believe the first step in fostering the sort of culture that can thrive in a VUCA world is to disseminate control. However, this comes with a caveat: when you take control away from traditional leadership, they can only respond by reaching for the command lever. As such, disseminating control and disseminating command come hand in hand. You can't foster continuous evolution if leadership is always kicking fish back into the sea.

This is not an exhaustive list of techniques that can be employed in the service of creating better Agile Governance. They are, however, a solid foundation. You need both Heart and Hands to be successful.

The only step left is for you to dive in yourself.

15

Get Out There and Make it Happen

Throughout this book we have referred to the writings and thoughts of Dr. Alistair Cockburn, creator of the Heart of Agile and one of the original seventeen co-authors of the *Agile Manifesto*, from which many of our ideas originate. Alistair has often discussed how much of a fluke of nature it was that a collection of curmudgeon software developers were the ones to decode the nature of knowledge work and what it took to work effectively, just in time for the Cambrian explosion of a digital-centric world.

The Agile Manifesto was signed in 2001—over 22 years ago. It's taken over two decades for the knowledge of how to work better and more humanely in the software and technology sphere to propagate and expand outward, beyond the coding of a website, to the management of people and systems. Yet, many organizations we work with are still working through foundational arguments such as:

> *"Agile isn't necessarily for everything."*
> *"Do you mean little 'a' or big 'A'?"*
> *"Agile is just for technology."*

These things are now table stakes, the bare minimum to get you into the game. Every technology is driven by software, so every company could be considered a technology company if you reflect on Marc Andreesen's famous quote, "Software is eating the world"[93].

When we butt up against these discussions, we're forced to ask: what industry do these people think they're in? What game do they think they're playing? We've also observed that, when people get caught up in debates about agility and its relevance to modern business, the arguments are rooted in ego, status, and control. Being able to respond quickly in a complex world requires people to give up certain types of control, and that's a difficult ask. We say yes to governance that controls the *way* decisions are made. Controlling the decisions themselves, though? That's a recipe for disaster.

Despite the resistance from certain organizations, we believe these concepts will continue to spread and percolate over time. There's a theory on the evolution of ideas and disruptive products that it takes thirty to forty years—maybe even fifty—from the genesis of a new idea to its commoditization. If we double back to Chapter 2 and the story of Copernicus (analogous to the story of the Customer Digital Revolution), you might recall that it wasn't until well after death that his ideas started to be broadly adopted, and then refuted. To follow from this thought, Steve Denning—to whom we have referred often throughout this book—has stated that agile and agility have become a management revolution over the last twenty years, especially in the last ten. As such, it's not surprising that such a gap in knowledge, experience, and adoption of agile exists in the governance of work.

There's no such thing as an overnight success, and we are only at the very start of the agile revolution. It might be true that most organizations will say, "We are agile," while only thinking of their technology functions. The 2022 State of Agile Report declares that,

---

[93] Andreesen.m, https://a16z.com/2011/08/20/why-software-is-eating-the-world/

amongst their respondents, there's an inherent bias amongst the agile community towards saying yes to questions like these: "80% of them are using agile as their predominant approach."

If we take these numbers at face value, it's fair to say that agile has crossed the chasm in this business and industry domain. However, outside the tech world, agile is still at the early majority stage, and so is business agility thinking. The industry has not yet explored how to inject agility into systems of governance, because it's only now becoming mainstream at an enterprise level.

Buying a Ferrari and Driving like a Lada

At the beginning of this book, we noted that not using agile in your governance systems was like being given the keys to a Ferrari and never getting out of first gear. You've got the car. You know how it can perform. You feel the power when the engine rumbles. You're stuck on a four-lane highway with back-to-back traffic, and all your focus goes into trying not to stall. Not to mention that as the driver of a red Ferrari everybody else on the highway is watching you. You've made the investments, you've got the stories to tell, the culture is shifting, and people can see you drive past! They want to be in the passenger seat beside you, going along for the ride. Yet you can't make that ride fulfill its true potential.

Your organization may already be that Ferrari. Maybe it's in the process of becoming one. However, you'll never be able to leverage the true power of your teams and leaders if you don't unshackle them from traditional governance. Regardless of where you are on your journey, it's important to observe Agile Governance principles: whether you're trying to strip back heavy governance processes preventing your teams from achieving what they could, or trying to introduce additional governance as your business grows up. To do so requires actively thinking about the system of work, the things you need to respond to internally, externally, and purposefully, and trying to do it all in a more flexible and adaptive way... while ensuring you comply with policies intended to protect the organization. It's no small task.

This challenge is at the heart of why and how we proposed and crafted the five stanchions of Agile Governance. The intent is to give you structure, guidance, and certainty, while allowing space for adaptation, emergence, and change—all things needed to survive in the digital age. To allow you to retain control, yet harness variability for your gain. We talk about it being scaffolding for you to build and design your own, bespoke operating model and system. That scaffolding, although built upon strong stanchions, still needs to be created in a way that suits the context of your organization and the customer's problems. To recap those stanchions:

1. **Conductive Leadership:** Everything starts with leadership, and 21st-century leadership is required to solve 21st century problems. Often you find an organization that has combined 19th century management with 20th century technology, and the combination completely fails when pitted against the problems of the modern age. As such, leaders need to rethink how they lead, and especially how they can move away from task and management focus to one more adaptive, guiding and enabling. To coaching rather than driving, so to speak. Conductive leadership is best envisioned through the metaphor of the leader as conductor of the orchestra. Yes, the musicians are following a score. Yes, your people are well trained and capable in their roles. Everyone is heading towards the same goal. Even so, a conductor is required to ensure everybody is fulfilling their role at the right point in time, individually or collectively. That's modern leadership. And it has the potential to produce magical music!

2. **Sensible Transparency:** The stanchion of Sensible Transparency is about how you can have the right information available at the right time to make the right decisions. At its heart, agile is about increasing the speed of decision-making and how quickly you can move an idea from the original idea holder to the idea executor. This is how we retool large, slow systems of work to be as nimble as their smaller competitors. We need this level of speed and transparency because, at the end of the day, customer value drives revenue and profitability, and both are under attack by disruptive players in every industry. This all must be achieved while remaining wary of creating too much transparency, which can overwhelm and introduce paralysis. Use this stanchion to find the balance between providing enough transparency to provide value, and inundating people with too many dashboards.

3. **Patterns of Work:** All work requiring more than one person to reach an outcome needs to be done collaboratively, which means you need to think about how you've designed that work. Everything is a process. Some schools of thought in the agile community believe process is a dirty word. Not true! We want processes that create consistency where needed but allow teams to describe how they want to operate locally to solve their problems. Leadership and management must make the decisions on setting those enabling constraints, while allowing points of variation that empower people to design, to the greatest extent possible, how they work to solve problems. In this manner, patterns of work are created that cascade throughout the organization and allow the other stanchions

to operate. It's a critical foundational stanchion to the successful injection of agility into your governance.

4. **Data Driven Reasoning:** Start everything with data, even if you're not sure of the accuracy! So long as you can get information that is directionally correct, will provide value, and you know will improve over time, it's beneficial and can drive useful conversations. At the very least, people will ask questions around the data itself and take ownership to improve it. Too many times now we've seen organizations failing to put the lens on themselves when it comes to performance, and consistently using data to inform decision-making. If you choose not to do this, you'll remain blind to whether or not you even have improved. You'll be unable to determine whether improvement efforts should continue, pause, pivot, or even stop. Standard operating procedures still remain highly valuable in some elements of work, particularly where problems are repeatable, or you intend to automate. The key is where and how to apply it to design your system of work so that the data you elevate from these different patterns has value.

5. **Humanity as the Cornerstone:** Continuing to keep people at the core is critical to the enablement of an agile organization, let alone injecting agility into your governance. Many organizations are moving towards customer centricity, putting customers at the heart of their strategy and development. When discussing humanity as the cornerstone of governance, we like to refer to Richard Branson. He's stated that Virgin is special because he puts people at the center; empowered, happy, and engaged staff who are appreciated for their work are the real

differentiators in a creative world. So, make sure that when you design your Agile Governance system, it's about enabling people as much as it is meeting the needs from a stakeholder, regulator, industry, or society. If in doubt, refer back to the opening statements of the Agile Manifesto: *"We are uncovering better ways of developing software by doing it and **helping others do it.**"*

The Stanchions create glue between these concepts and your own governance. That doesn't mean that you can incorporate stanchion-thinking and then stand still. Continuous improvement is a key aspect of Agile Governance. Yes, the stanchions are fixed. They have solid foundations you should organize around. However, the world doesn't stand still, so you need to make sure that your approach allows for flexibility when something inevitably shifts.

That's why what we've given you a selection of industry practices around how you might inspect and adapt the processes and stanchions to suit your organization. As the environment moves and things change, you should be constantly re-visiting what you have put in place and considering how best to allow your Agile Governance ecosystem to meet your needs. Evolving practices and processes are at the Heart of Agile, and that extends to Agile Governance.

What is normal?

The next normal is coming. In fact, by the time you've recognized the "next normal," it's probably already the current normal. If you want to be ready for these continuous waves of change, you need to seriously examine your governance now! To thrive, you'll need to consider an intentional organizational design that creates or enhances collaborative connective tissues in order to enable communication, information flow, and increased speed of directional decisions.

With the advent of COVID-19, we saw that our idea of normal can be disrupted at any moment. In fact, there is no normal. There is only change. Even if you think you're stabilized and comfortable, something or someone will eventually disrupt it. The modern VUCA world won't allow you to paddle in place.

So, when it comes to change, you can make changes piecemeal, or you can look at how the system is governed as a whole. Agile Governance enables this. However, only you can turn it from theory into reality.

Get out there. Examine your systems of governance critically. Look at them through the lens of the five stanchions.

Remember:
Don't apply governance to your agile.
Apply agility to your governance!

ACKNOWLEDGEMENTS

We would like to express our deep gratitude to the founders of Elabor8, Nam Huynh, Paul Velonis, and Andrew Blain, for affording us the opportunity to begin refining our ideas and perspectives. For furthering that journey, we would also like to extend our gratitude to John Tooth, the CEO of the Remote Agility Framework, and Andrew Blain, the founder of the Remote Agility Framework, who provided us with the opportunity to build on those ideas on an international stage.

We have learned from, worked closely with, and stayed in close contact with Alistair Cockburn over the years. His thinking and approach to people and work, his openness and willingness to always have a conversation about agile is something that we deeply cherish.

Dr. Amy Silver is another person whom we have taken a lot of our thinking on how to create an agile environment by encouraging people to be brave and face change. She has also provided some guidance on how we go about getting to this published stage, giving her time freely, and we thank her for that.

Our thanks go to Craig Smith, who encouraged us to take the talk we had presented at Agile Australia and write this book from it. Craig and Tony grew up in agile together, and he has not only been a friend and confidant to us; without his review and encouragement, this book would never have reached completion.

Phil Abernathy, we have learned so many lessons from you both in agility and how to apply it in an organizational sense. It was you that provided the catalyst of thinking about looking at the entire system and how it is governed. We are eternally grateful for your countenance and mentoring over the years.

The thinking of the wonderful Esther Derby has influenced us greatly. Having had the opportunity to talk, work, and interview her over the last few years, we have learned much about the thinking of the organizational system as a whole and the integral interactions that enable and disable the governing of the system as a whole. We are forever grateful.

We have spent time, though not nearly enough, over a cold beer in a Fitzroy pub talking about how the Business Agility Institute shapes out organizational agile thinking with Evan Leybourn, the co-founder of the Global Business Agility Institute. Evan's unique and somewhat rare grasp on what makes enterprise-level agility has been something we draw from and look forward to contributing back to!

We can't forget to recognize who we rate as one of the true fathers of Australian agile, the erstwhile Craig Brown. Craig is the co-founder of the Australian Lean Agile Systems Thinking Conference and has been in this domain for eons. If you ever want to test an idea, ask Craig. He'll have a view or an opinion that invariably gets you thinking more and helps shape your direction. He is another one of those folk who will always have time for a beer and a conversation.

The Australian agile community is one of the most open and sharing communities to be found anywhere. It truly is a broad church where any ideas can be surfaced and trialled, and generally any person involved is willing to share their story of agile transformation—what worked, what didn't, and what did we learn? Interacting with this group has broadened our horizons and provided us with the ability to give back, and it's one that we have chosen to be a close part of for well over a decade. Special thanks to Chris Chan, Rachel Slattery, Ed Wong, Alexandra Stokes, Peter Lam, Steven Lawrence, Paul Caon, Adina Thavsin, Renee Troughton, Dave Martin, James McMennamin, Phil Grech, Martin Kearns, Sandy Mamoli, Shane Hastie, Farnaz Vahab, Nikola Peters, and Nish Mahanty.

A big thank you goes to Chris Hayes-Kossman for helping us find our writing style, get our ideas out, and keep us moving forward.

Over the years of agile going from a revolution in software delivery to now enterprise management, the one global author who has kept his finger on the change is Steve Denning. We drew on his research as a source for where the agile market trends towards.

In our view, the leading thinker globally on complexity theory in organizations is Dave Snowden, the founder and chief scientific officer of The Cynefin Company, specializing in complexity and sensemaking. Reading the paper he co-published in 2007, *A Leader's Framework for Decision-Making*, was a pivotal point in how we view how organizations solve different types of problems and how leaders need different styles and approaches to navigate those problems. We have referenced and adopted the Cynefin Framework extensively over the years.

Brian Rivera, John Turner, and Nigel Thurlow are the co-authors of *The Flow System*. Their approach to enabling systems of work to better deliver customer value, emerging from the roots of the Toyota Production System and Lean, is something we resonate with.

We have had the pleasure over the years of reading, interviewing, and talking with Stephen Bungay, L. David Marquet, and Christopher Avery, and it would be remiss not to acknowledge their influences on our thought processes.

We can't end our acknowledgements without recognising the other sixteen original authors of *The Agile Manifesto*, alongside Alistair Cockburn. We are reasonably confident that the gathering in February 2001 at The Lodge at Snowbird ski resort in the Wasatch mountains of Utah didn't predict the impact they would have, not only on how to develop software but also on how to run organizations that are filled with knowledge workers. And we are forever grateful that they did.

We truly stand on the shoulders of giants.

ABOUT THE AUTHORS

Tony Ponton

My career has been eclectic, to say the least. I left a career in the music industry and worked in many different jobs before landing in a large banking and insurance organization in the early nineties. I fulfilled many roles for the organization: trainer, software tester, and business analyst, before a stroke of luck in the late 90s introduced me to agile. That organization became Australia's premier poster-child for agile transformation.

I was extremely lucky to share that journey with a group of amazing agilists whom I learned much from. Within that period, I spent my time coaching large programs such as an Internet Banking Rebuild, and a Banking Replacement Program. While doing so, I learned much about agile and governance.

Since that time, I have been active as a contributor and leader in the Australian and global agile communities and am one of the co-creators, co-authors, and vice-president of "The Remote Agility Framework".

In between helping organizations change the world of work, I co-chair one of the world's first and premier agile podcasts, *The Agile Revolution*, host the YouTube channel *All the Remote Things*, the YouTube chat show *@talkingremote*, and serve as a Heart of Agile guide for the global Heart of Agile movement.

Phil Gadzinksi

I have truly had a diverse career and worked in various industries and types of roles, with my first true job being in the Australian Army way back in 1991. After university, in the early 2000s, I found myself working at a large bank in Australia. It was embarking on their first experiments with the adoption of agile methods in the technology space, and looking to expand that to project delivery. I was fortunate enough to be in a position to take on the role of project manager. The success of the project was amazing and somewhat legendary, and it set up the next rounds of agile adoption within that organization. I learned by doing, without actually understanding the theory. It was only over the next fifteen years that I truly learned what agile *is* and *needs*. It is said that success can be a bad teacher. I've found that applies to myself. Every scenario is different—you really have to learn and rely on the people around you to be successful.

I moved to agile program delivery, software delivery, and eventually agile transformations, enabling agile as a "thing" to move out of the technology domain and into the wild. I've been fortunate to work in large organizations, most recently with a global company trying to support the uplift of capability across 80,000 people and seventeen countries. I have found my niche in how we adopt agility across the organization, and over that time I have found that the key constraints to success are not agile itself but rather the existing system that works around it and rarely gets tackled as part of the change journey.

I have worked extensively with Alistair Cockburn, one of the co-signatories of the original agile manifesto, including in the creation of the Heart of Agile, which is his approach to getting agile back to the essence of agility, including being one of the first globally recognized guides, of which I am still active. Tony and I are both Global Heart of Agile Guides. Most recently, with Andrew Blain and team, I helped to co-create the initial Remote Agility Framework. I was also recently recognized as an Executive Guide in Operating Model Design.

Tony and I have worked together over many years; we've contributed to and given many talks, particularly on this topic of Agile Governance, and we are both actively engaged and recognized as leaders in the agile industry in Australia. This book is based on a series of talks we give at agile conferences, as well as a series of blog posts we wrote to provide our view and early thinking around how you inject agility into governance. It is humbling to be able to write and produce this with Tony, who I count as one of the most authentic and engaging Agilists you will ever meet.

Book reviews can make or break a book.
If you liked what you read today, and found the information helpful, please
do consider posting a review on your favorite forum.

Govern Agility is available at governagility.com.au
and all major online retailers—print and ebook

For business book production contact Hawkeye Press, an imprint of hawkeyebooks.com.au

www.ingramcontent.com/pod-product-compliance
Lightning Source LLC
Chambersburg PA
CBHW020608270326
41927CB00005B/234